I0528977

GLENN KENNEDY

365 Affirmations

Cultivating Mindfulness, Motivation, and Success

Copyright © 2024 by Glenn Kennedy

All rights reserved. No part of this publication may be
reproduced, stored or transmitted in any form or by any
means, electronic, mechanical, photocopying, recording,
scanning, or otherwise without written permission from the
publisher. It is illegal to copy this book, post it to a website, or
distribute it by any other means without permission.

First edition

This book was professionally typeset on Reedsy.
Find out more at reedsy.com

Dedication:

To Mom and Dad,

Your love and guidance have shaped me into the seeker I am today. From childhood, you provided me with the tools of curiosity and resilience, nurturing my thirst for knowledge. Your wisdom has been my compass, teaching me kindness, empathy, and the pursuit of truth. This book is a tribute to your love and inspiration, reflecting the seeds you planted that now flourish in me.

With love,
Your Son

"To the seeker of truth and transformation: may these words be your guiding stars and your steady compass, leading you to the shores of your greatest self."

–Glenn Kennedy

Contents

Foreword

As I sit down to pen the foreword for "365 Daily Affirmations: Cultivating Mindfulness, Motivation, and Success," I am struck by the transformative power that lies within the simple act of daily affirmation. In this remarkable book, Glenn has distilled the essence of a profound truth: that the words we repeat to ourselves have the power to shape our thoughts, actions, and ultimately, our lives.

Having known Glenn for many years, I've witnessed firsthand his dedication to the art and science of personal development. Their journey, marked by both triumphs and challenges, has imbued them with a deep understanding of the human spirit's resilience and potential. This book is a testament to their commitment to sharing that wisdom with others.

Each page of this book is a stepping stone on a path towards greater self-awareness, motivation, and success. The affirmations are carefully crafted, designed not only to uplift but also to challenge the reader to delve deeper into their own psyche and discover their true potential.

What sets this book apart is its universal applicability. Regardless of where you find yourself in life's journey, these affirmations offer a beacon of light, guiding you towards a more mindful and fulfilling existence. Whether you are looking to overcome personal obstacles, achieve specific goals, or simply cultivate a more positive outlook, these daily affirmations serve as a powerful tool in your arsenal.

As you turn each page, I encourage you to embrace the affirmations with an open heart and a reflective mind. Allow them to resonate with your personal experiences and aspirations. Remember, the true power of these affirmations lies in your commitment to integrating them into your daily life.

"365 Daily Affirmations: Cultivating Mindfulness, Motivation, and Success" is more than a book; it is a daily companion on your journey towards personal growth and fulfillment. May you find in these pages the inspiration and strength to create the life you desire and deserve.

With warm regards,

Beatrice Vale

Preface

Welcome to "365 Daily Affirmations: Cultivating Mindfulness, Motivation, and Success." Before you embark on this year-long journey of personal transformation, I'd like to share a few thoughts that lay the foundation for the pages that follow.

This book was born from a simple yet profound realization: the words we tell ourselves shape our reality. In my years of exploring personal development, I have witnessed the incredible power of affirmations in shaping thoughts, attitudes, and life trajectories. Each affirmation in this book is a distilled essence of wisdom, crafted to inspire, challenge, and guide you towards a more fulfilling life.

The affirmations you will encounter are more than just positive statements. They are invitations to engage with your deepest selves, to confront your limiting beliefs, and to kindle the spark of possibility that resides within you. This book is designed for those who seek to cultivate a mindful approach to life, to foster motivation in pursuit of their goals, and to carve a path of success, however they define it.

As you journey through these pages day by day, I encourage you to approach each affirmation with an open heart and a reflective mind. Allow yourself the space to ponder, to feel, and to apply these words in the context of your own life. Some affirmations may resonate deeply with you, while others may challenge your existing perceptions. Embrace this as part of the journey.

I have endeavored to make this book a companion for anyone, irrespective of where you are in your life's journey. Whether you are looking to make a significant change, seeking comfort during challenging times, or simply wish to start each day with a positive thought, these affirmations are here to support you.

Thank you for choosing to embark on this journey with me. May the affirmations in this book light your way each day, and may you find within its pages the inspiration and strength to transform your life.

With hope and warmth,

Glenn

Acknowledgement

As I reflect on the journey that led to the creation of "365 Daily Affirmations: Cultivating Mindfulness, Motivation, and Success," I am filled with profound gratitude for the many individuals who have contributed to the realization of this book.

Firstly, I extend my deepest appreciation to my family, whose unwavering support and belief in my vision have been the bedrock of my perseverance. Your love and encouragement have been my constant source of strength.

To my friends, who have been both my sounding board and my cheerleaders, thank you for your invaluable insights and endless encouragement. Your faith in my work has been a vital source of motivation.

I owe a debt of gratitude to the mentors and teachers who have guided me throughout my personal and professional journey. Your wisdom and teachings have been instrumental in shaping my understanding of personal development and the power of affirmations.

A special thank you to my editorial team, whose expertise and dedication transformed my manuscript into the book it is today. Your keen eyes and insightful suggestions have been invaluable.

I am also grateful to the design and production teams for bringing the visual aspect of this book to life with such care and creativity. Your talent and attention to detail have made this book not just a source of wisdom, but also a work of art.

To the countless individuals who shared their personal stories and experiences with me, thank you for your trust and openness. Your journeys have been a source of inspiration and have deeply enriched the content of this book.

And finally, to you, the reader, for embarking on this journey with me. This book was written with the hope that it would touch lives and inspire change. Thank you for allowing me the opportunity to be a part of your journey towards mindfulness, motivation, and success.

With heartfelt thanks,

Glenn

1

Foundations of Affirmations

Understanding Affirmations

In a world often clouded with negativity and doubt, affirmations stand as a powerful antidote, offering a path to positive transformation. These simple, yet impactful statements are designed to affirm and reinforce the innate strengths, values, and aspirations of an individual, countering the barrage of negative influences that one may encounter in daily life.

The practice of affirmations is more than mere repetition of positive words; it is an act of instilling hope, confidence, and positivity into one's very being. In a society where negative news, self-doubt, and criticism are prevalent, affirmations serve as a personal shield, protecting and fortifying the mind against these external negativities. They empower individuals to shift their focus from external chaos to internal peace, from uncertainty to clarity, and from fear to courage.

The transformative power of affirmations is profound. Regularly engaging in this practice can lead to remarkable changes in one's mindset and overall quality of life. Where once there might have been self-doubt, affirmations cultivate self-belief; where there was fear, they foster courage; where there was despair, they sow seeds of hope. This shift in mindset brought about by affirmations can lead to tangible changes in one's life – improved mental health, enhanced self-esteem, better stress management, and a more optimistic outlook on life.

In essence, affirmations are not just phrases to be spoken; they are powerful declarations of one's truth and potential. They are a conscious choice to focus on the positive, to nurture the mind with thoughts that uplift and inspire. In doing so, affirmations become a vital tool in navigating the complexities of modern life, transforming not only how one views themselves but also how they interact with and perceive the world.

Historical and Cultural Perspectives

Affirmations, though widely popularized in modern self-help cultures, have deep historical and cultural roots that showcase their transformative impact through the ages. In ancient times, affirmations were often intertwined with spiritual practices. For instance, in Vedic traditions of India, mantras—precursors to modern affirmations—were used not just for spiritual enlightenment but also for practical purposes, like improving health and attracting prosperity. These mantras brought about a heightened sense of inner peace and harmony, influencing both the individual and the community's well-being.

Similarly, in Ancient Egypt, the power of spoken word was believed to bring about actual change in reality. Pharaohs and priests used carefully crafted affirmations in their rituals, believing these words could command the gods' favor, protect against evil, and ensure the prosperity of their reign. This illustrates how affirmations were not only a spiritual tool but also a means of societal governance and order.

In the West, during the Middle Ages and Renaissance, affirmations found their place in Christian prayers and declarations. The practice of daily affirmations by monks and nuns, often centered around themes of humility, service, and devotion, brought significant shifts in their mental states and perceptions, fostering communities deeply rooted in these values.

The New Thought Movement in the 19th and early 20th centuries marked a pivotal shift, where affirmations transitioned from religious contexts into the realm of personal development and psychology. Pioneers like Émile Coué promoted the use of positive self-talk for mental and physical health improvement, a practice that led to noticeable changes in individuals' self-esteem and well-being.

Throughout history, the consistent thread has been the transformative power of affirmations. Whether in ancient rituals or modern therapy sessions, affirmations have served as tools for personal and societal transformation, bringing about changes in mindset, health, and even social structures. They demonstrate the enduring belief across cultures and epochs in the power of words to reshape reality and influence human destiny.

Psychological Impact of Positive Affirmations

The practice of positive affirmations has a profound psychological impact, particularly in the realms of mental health and therapeutic interventions. Notably, in dealing with illnesses such as depression, affirmations can serve as a powerful tool for fostering a positive mindset and alleviating symptoms.

In individuals suffering from depression, negative thought patterns are often deeply ingrained, creating a cycle of despair and hopelessness. Positive affirmations act as a counterforce to these negative thoughts. By regularly repeating affirmations that emphasize self-worth, hope, and inner strength, individuals can start to rewire their thought processes. This practice gradually shifts the focus from negative beliefs to a more optimistic outlook, contributing to an improved emotional state.

Clinical studies have shown that the use of positive affirmations can lead to changes in the brain's neural pathways. These changes are associated with greater feelings of self-empowerment and control, which are crucial in combating depressive symptoms. Furthermore, affirmations can boost self-esteem, reduce stress, and increase resilience against daily pressures, all of which are essential factors in managing depression.

Beyond the individual, affirmations can also enhance the therapeutic process. When used alongside traditional treatments like cognitive-behavioral therapy, affirmations can reinforce the positive messages and coping strategies introduced by mental health professionals. This synergy can accelerate the healing process, aiding individuals in overcoming the challenges posed by depression more effectively.

In essence, the psychological impact of positive affirmations is significant, especially for those battling mental illnesses like depression. They provide a simple yet powerful means to break free from negative thought patterns, instill a sense of hope, and pave the way towards mental well-being and recovery.

Setting the Mindset for Daily Practice

Establishing a daily practice of affirmations is not merely about reciting words; it's about cultivating a mindset that transcends the practice itself, influencing various aspects of life. This mindset is characterized by intentionality, awareness, and consistency, forming the bedrock for profound personal transformation.

Firstly, intentional practice is key. By choosing affirmations that resonate deeply with personal goals and values, individuals can create a powerful alignment between their words and their life's direction. This intentionality ensures that the affirmations are not just recited, but are deeply felt and believed, making them more effective.

Moreover, the discipline of daily practice fosters a broader sense of awareness. Regular engagement with affirmations heightens mindfulness, making individuals more attuned to their thoughts and feelings. This increased awareness often spills over into other areas of life, leading to more mindful interactions, decision-making, and responses to life's challenges.

Consistency in practicing affirmations also brings about a shift in mindset from a fixed to a growth-oriented perspective. As individuals repeat positive and empowering statements, they start to internalize these beliefs, which in turn enhances their self-esteem and resilience. This change in mindset is transformative, influencing not just personal self-perception but also how one engages with the world.

In essence, the daily practice of affirmations is a journey of aligning one's thoughts with their desired reality. It's about creating a positive ripple effect that extends beyond the moments of practice, influencing thoughts, behaviors, and actions in all facets of life. It's a commitment to nurturing a positive and growth-oriented mindset, a crucial step towards achieving mindfulness, motivation, and success.

Laying the Foundations of Transformation

As we conclude the first chapter of our journey into the world of affirmations, it's important to reflect on the foundational role they play in personal growth and transformation. This chapter has introduced the concept of daily affirmations, unraveling their potential to shape our mindset, influence our emotions, and guide our actions towards desired outcomes.

We have explored how affirmations are much more than just positive statements; they are tools for self-empowerment. By deliberately choosing words that resonate with our deepest aspirations and values, we begin to lay the groundwork for a positive change in our lives. The affirmations serve as reminders of our capabilities, goals, and the type of person we aspire to become.

The key takeaway from this chapter is the understanding that affirmations are a starting point. They initiate a dialogue with our inner selves, opening us up to possibilities and perspectives that we might not have considered before. By repeating these affirmations, we reinforce positive beliefs and attitudes, setting the stage for further growth and development.

As we move forward, let's carry the insights gained from this chapter with the understanding that our journey is just beginning. The true power of affirmations will be realized as we integrate them into our daily lives, allowing them to shape our thoughts and actions in meaningful ways. The journey ahead is one of exploration, learning, and growth, with affirmations as our guiding light.

2

Integrating Affirmations into Daily Life

Creating a Daily Affirmation Routine

Establishing a regular routine for daily affirmations is pivotal in transforming them from mere words into powerful habits that shape your mindset and actions. Here's a guide to creating an effective affirmation routine, tailored for both beginners and those more experienced:

For Beginners - Laying the Foundation:

1. Select a Specific Time: Begin by dedicating a specific time each day for your affirmations. Mornings are often preferred as they set a positive tone for the day ahead. Consistency at this time helps anchor the habit.

2. Find Your Space: Choose a quiet spot where you can be undisturbed. This could be a cozy corner in your home or a

peaceful outdoor setting. A consistent location reinforces the habit.

3. Start Simple: Begin with 2-3 affirmations. Choose statements that resonate with your current life situation and aspirations. Simple, meaningful affirmations are easier to internalize.

4. Repeat and Reflect: Say your affirmations slowly, reflecting on each word. Feel the emotion behind the statements. This deepens the connection between the words and your subconscious.

For the Experienced - Deepening the Practice:

1. Vary Your Timings: Experiment with practicing affirmations at different times of the day to understand how it impacts different activities and moods.

2. Diversify Your Space: Change your environment occasionally. Practicing in a park or during a quiet moment at work can integrate affirmations more deeply into everyday life.

3. Customize and Expand: Develop more personalized affirmations that address specific areas of your life you are working on. Add more affirmations to your routine as you become comfortable.

4. Combine with Other Practices: Incorporate affirmations into your meditation, journaling, or during exercise. This enhances the holistic impact of the affirmations on your lifestyle.

A regular routine is pivotal in habit formation as it provides structure and consistency, two key elements in making any practice an integral part of your life. For affirmations, this routine not only instills them into your daily life but also continuously reinforces the positive mindset they aim to develop.

Overcoming Challenges and Common Misconceptions

Navigating through the practice of affirmations often involves confronting skepticism and dispelling common misconceptions. Understanding and overcoming these challenges is essential for harnessing the full potential of affirmations.

Challenge: Skepticism and Expectation of Immediate Results

- Nature of Challenge: Many people approach affirmations with a degree of skepticism, doubting their efficacy. This skepticism is often coupled with an expectation for quick, visible results, leading to disillusionment when changes aren't immediately apparent.
   - Overcoming Strategy: Emphasize the gradual nature of affirmations. They work subtly and require time to effect change in thought patterns and attitudes. Consistency and patience are key.
   - Example of Transformation: Consider a software engineer, initially skeptical, who began using affirmations as a part of a wellness challenge at work. Despite initialdoubts, he committed to the practice, repeating affirmations focused on stress management and work-life balance. Over several weeks, he started noticing a shift in his reactions to workplace stressors and an improved ability to maintain a calm demeanor in high-pressure situations. His initial skepticism turned into belief

as he experienced firsthand the gradual yet impactful change affirmations brought to his professional and personal life.

Challenge: Misconception of Unrealistic Optimism

- Nature of Challenge: A common misconception is that affirmations are just overly optimistic or even a form of self-deception.
  - Overcoming Strategy: Affirmations should be grounded in realism and personal truth. They are most effective when they resonate with one's genuine aspirations and are perceived as attainable.
  - Example of Transformation: Take the case of a writer who initially felt affirmations were too fanciful. However, upon tailoring affirmations to her specific aspirations, such as overcoming writer's block and enhancing creativity, she began to see a change. Her affirmations felt more genuine and led to a noticeable increase in productivity and creative output.

Challenge: Belief in a One-Size-Fits-All Approach

- Nature of Challenge: Another misconception is that the same set of affirmations works universally for everyone.
  - Overcoming Strategy: Personalization is crucial for the efficacy of affirmations. They should align with individual goals, challenges, and belief systems.
  - Example of Transformation: A retired athlete, struggling with a new life away from competitive sports, initially used general affirmations with little effect. When he shifted to affirmations that focused on his new goals of coaching and

mentoring young athletes, he found a renewed sense of purpose and motivation.

In overcoming these challenges and misconceptions, individuals can realize the true value of affirmations as a tool for personal growth and mindset transformation. By approaching affirmations with patience, realism, and a personalized touch, their effectiveness in fostering positive change becomes increasingly evident.

Personalizing Affirmations for Maximum Impact

To harness the full power of affirmations, personalization is key. Tailoring affirmations to align with individual goals, experiences, and aspirations ensures they resonate more deeply and are more effective in bringing about desired changes.

Understanding Personal Goals and Values:

- Start by reflecting on your personal goals, values, and areas of life you wish to improve or change. This self-reflection forms the foundation for creating affirmations that are truly meaningful to you.

Crafting Unique Affirmations:

- Use specific, positive language that speaks directly to your aspirations. For instance, if you're aiming to become more confident in public speaking, an affirmation like "I am calm and articulate in my presentations" can be more impactful than a generic "I am confident."

Incorporating Emotional Resonance:

- Affirmations should evoke a positive emotional response. Choose words that make you feel empowered, hopeful, or peaceful. The emotional charge behind the words is what gives them power.

Example of Personalization:

- A teacher looking to bring more patience and understanding into her classroom might create an affirmation like, "I approach each student with patience and understanding, recognizing their unique needs and potential." This personalized affirmation directly addresses her specific situation and goals, making it more potent than a general statement about patience.

Regular Review and Adaptation:

- As your life changes and evolves, so should your affirmations. Regularly review and adjust them to ensure they continue to align with your current goals and circumstances. This keeps the practice relevant and effective.

Personalizing affirmations is about making them a mirror of your unique journey and aspirations. By crafting affirmations that are closely aligned with your personal narrative, they become powerful tools that can significantly influence your mindset and help you achieve your specific goals.

Success Stories and Case Studies

This section presents a series of genuine success stories and case studies, highlighting how individuals from various backgrounds have effectively used affirmations in their lives:

1. Sarah, New York City - Overcoming Public Speaking Anxiety: Sarah, a marketing manager in New York City, utilized affirmations to conquer her fear of public speaking. Regularly affirming "I am confident and articulate in expressing my ideas," she noticed a marked improvement in her presentation skills, leading to successful pitches and enhanced leadership roles.

2. David, San Francisco - Career Shift: David, a software engineer in San Francisco, aspired to transition to graphic

design. By affirming "My creativity is recognized and valued," he bolstered his confidence, built an impressive portfolio, and successfully switched careers.

3. Emily, Chicago - Marathon Training: As an amateur runner in Chicago, Emily used the affirmation, "Each stride strengthens and empowers me," during her marathon training. This helped her complete the marathon with a commendable time, surpassing her expectations.

4. Carlos, Miami - Recovery from Injury: Professional dancer Carlos from Miami faced a challenging recovery after an ankle injury. His affirmation, "My body heals quickly and efficiently," complemented his rehabilitation and led to a quicker return to dancing.

5. Aisha, Toronto - Building Self-Confidence: Aisha, a high school teacher in Toronto, used affirmations to enhance her self-confidence in classroom management. "I am a capable and respected educator," she affirmed daily, leading to improved confidence, more effective teaching, and positive feedback from students.

6. Mark, London - Financial Stability: Facing financial challenges, Mark, a small business owner in London, adopted the affirmation, "I make wise and beneficial financial decisions." This new mindset resulted in better financial management and growth for his business.

7. Elena and Tom, Sydney - Relationship Improvement: To address communication issues, Elena and Tom from Sydney

started using the affirmation, "We communicate with understanding and respect." This practice fostered better listening and empathy, strengthening their relationship.

8. Raj, Bangalore - Academic Success: Raj, a university student in Bangalore, used affirmations to overcome academic anxieties. By affirming "I am focused, intelligent, and capable of excelling in my studies," he improved his concentration and academic performance.

9. Glenn, Los Angeles - Acting Career Enhancement: Glenn, an aspiring actor in Los Angeles, faced challenges in his acting career. He began affirming, "I am talented and my performances captivate audiences," which helped him approach auditions with more confidence. This shift in mindset led to notable roles in theater productions and a gradual rise in his acting career.

These stories showcase the transformative power of affirmations in different aspects of life, from personal growth and career changes to relationship enhancement and creative pursuits. Each individual's journey underscores the effectiveness of personalized affirmations in achieving specific goals and overcoming unique challenges.

Mastering the Art of Affirmation Integration

As we conclude Chapter 2, we reflect on the essential role of integrating affirmations into our everyday lives. This chapter has provided a deeper understanding of how to make affirmations more than just words, transforming them into actionable beliefs that positively influence our daily experiences and behaviors.

We have explored various methods to effectively embed affirmations into our routines, from incorporating them into morning rituals to repeating them during moments of reflection throughout the day. By doing so, we ensure that these affirmations become a consistent and powerful force, driving us towards our goals and shaping our mindset.

The significance of making affirmations personal and meaningful has been a key focus. Tailoring affirmations to our individual aspirations, challenges, and life circumstances enhances their relevance and impact. When affirmations resonate deeply with us, they become powerful motivators and reminders of our capabilities and potential.

Additionally, this chapter highlighted the importance of persistence and belief in the process. The regular practice of affirmations requires dedication and patience, as the transformation they bring about may not be immediate. However, with continuous effort and belief in their power, affirmations can lead to significant shifts in our thoughts, emotions, and actions.

In summary, Chapter 2 has laid the groundwork for turning affirmations from simple statements into dynamic tools for personal growth and change. As we progress on this journey, the consistent and mindful application of these affirmations will be instrumental in guiding us towards realizing our full potential and achieving our desired life changes.

3

Make a Difference with Your Review
Unlock the Power of Generosity

Cultivating a better self is the key to unlocking a brighter future."
- Glenn Kennedy

Transforming your mindset and empowering yourself doesn't just benefit you; it has a ripple effect on the world around you. In the world of affirmations, we're on a journey to transform ourselves, one thought at a time, and it's a journey worth sharing.

So, I have a question for you...

Would you help someone discover the incredible power of daily affirmations, even if you never got credit for it?

Who is this person you ask? They are like you—seeking growth, motivation, and success. They may be unsure of where to begin, and your review can be their guiding light.

Our mission is to make the practice of daily affirmations accessible to everyone, and your support is invaluable to achieving that mission. And, the only way for us to accomplish this mission is by reaching as many individuals as possible.

This is where your generosity can make a significant impact. Most people value the opinions of others, especially when it comes to personal development. So here's my request on behalf of someone who's looking to transform their life:

Please help that individual by leaving a review for this book.

Your act of kindness costs nothing and takes just a minute of your time, but it can change a fellow seeker's life forever. Your review could help...

...one more person find inner peace.
    ...one more dream become a reality.
    ...one more individual achieve their goals.
    ...one more soul discover the power within.

To make a real difference and help others on their journey, all you have to do is...and it takes less than 60 seconds...
    leave a review.

Simply scan the QR code below to share your thoughts:

https://www.amazon.com/review/review-your-purchases/?asin=B0CSX8RY8K

SCAN ME!

If you feel inspired to empower someone else on their path to personal growth, you are my kind of person. Welcome to the community of seekers dedicated to positive change.

I'm thrilled to share this transformative journey with you, and in the upcoming chapters, you'll find tools and insights that can change your life in remarkable ways.

Thank you for your generosity, and let's continue spreading positivity and growth together.

With gratitude,
   Glenn

PS – Fun fact: By helping others, you become more valuable to them. If you believe this book can empower someone you know, consider sharing it with them as a gesture of goodwill.

4

365 Daily Affirmations

This chapter provides a carefully curated collection of 365 affirmations, each accompanied by a brief, insightful explanation or inspirational note. These affirmations are organized thematically and are listed starting from January 1st. However, they are designed to be flexible and applicable at any start date in any year, ensuring their relevance and effectiveness for every individual at any time.

January - New Beginnings: Focusing on setting intentions, embracing new opportunities, and starting the year with a fresh perspective.

Theme: Mindfulness
- January 1st: "I welcome this new day with peace and joy in my heart."
- Note: Begin your year with an affirmation that sets a tone of calmness and positivity for the days ahead.

Theme: Motivation
- January 2nd: "Today, I take a step towards my dreams and goals."
- Note: Let the start of the year be a catalyst for action towards your aspirations.

Theme: Personal Growth
- January 3rd: "I am open to learning and growing every day."
- Note: Embrace each day as an opportunity for self-improvement and knowledge.

Theme: Success
- January 4th: "Success is my natural state; I attract it effortlessly."
- Note: Instill a belief in your innate ability to achieve and attract success.

Theme: Mindfulness
- January 5th: "I am fully present in every moment of my life."

- Note: Encourage yourself to experience each moment deeply, enhancing mindfulness.

Theme: Motivation

-January 6th: "Obstacles are merely steps to my ultimate success."

-Note: Reframe challenges as stepping stones, fueling your motivation to overcome them.

Theme: Personal Growth

-January 7th: "Every experience enriches my personal journey."

- Note: Value each experience as a contributor to your growth and development.

Theme: Success

- January 8th: "I am deserving of success and all the good that life offers."

- Note: Cultivate a mindset that recognizes and accepts success as a deserved part of your life.

Theme: Mindfulness

- January 9: "I cherish the beauty in each moment."

- Note: Find and appreciate the beauty in the everyday, it's there if you look for it.

Theme: Mindfulness

- January 10: "My mind is calm, my heart is at peace."

- Note: Cultivate inner peace as a foundation for your day.

Theme: Motivation

- January 11: "I am a powerhouse; I can achieve anything I set my mind to."
- Note: Recognize your inner strength and channel it towards your goals.

Theme: Motivation
- January 12: "Today, I embrace challenges as stepping stones to success."
- Note: Treat every challenge as an opportunity to learn and grow stronger.

Theme: Personal Growth
- January 13: "Every day, I evolve into a better version of myself."
- Note: Embrace the journey of continuous self-improvement.

- January 14: "I learn from the past, live in the present, and plan for the future."
- Note: Balance your time and thoughts across all aspects of time for well-rounded growth.

Theme: Success
- January 15: "I attract success by being true to myself."
- Note: Authenticity is a magnet for success in all areas of life.

Theme: Success
- January 16: "Every small success is a building block to greater achievement."
- Note: Acknowledge and celebrate small victories; they are crucial steps on your path to success.

Theme: Mindfulness

- January 17: "I am grateful for the abundance in my life."

- Note: Acknowledge and appreciate the abundance that surrounds you, enhancing your sense of gratitude.

Theme: Motivation

- January 18: "I possess the determination and drive to succeed."

- Note: Affirm your inner strength and determination to overcome obstacles and achieve success.

Theme: Personal Growth

- January 19: "I embrace new experiences as opportunities for growth."

- Note: View each new experience as a chance to learn something valuable about yourself and the world.

Theme: Success

- January 20: "My actions create constant prosperity."

- Note: Understand that your actions are powerful catalysts for success and prosperity.

Theme: Mindfulness

- January 21: "I am in harmony with the rhythm of my own life."

- Note: Feel the flow of your life and align yourself with its natural rhythm for peace and clarity.

Theme: Motivation

- January 22: "Challenges inspire me to push my boundaries."

- Note: Let challenges be a source of inspiration, pushing you to expand your limits and grow.

Theme: Personal Growth
   - January 23: "I am resilient, adaptable, and strong."
   - Note: Affirm your resilience and ability to adapt to change, key qualities for personal growth.

Theme: Success
   - January 24: "I celebrate every goal I achieve."
   - Note: Take time to celebrate your achievements, no matter how small, as each is a step towards greater success.

Theme: Mindfulness
   - January 25: "Today, I find joy in small moments."
   - Note: Embrace the joy in simple, everyday experiences, enhancing your mindfulness.

Theme: Motivation
   - January 26: "I am driven by my vision and commitment to my goals."
   - Note: Let your clear vision and commitment be the driving force behind your actions today.

Theme: Personal Growth
   - January 27: "I am a work in progress, and that is okay."
   - Note: Acknowledge and accept that personal growth is an ongoing process and be kind to yourself along the journey.

Theme: Success
   - January 28: "Success to me means living according to my values."

- Note: Define success on your own terms, aligning it with your personal values and beliefs.

Theme: Mindfulness
- January 29: "I observe my thoughts and actions without judgment."
- Note: Practice observing your thoughts and actions mindfully, fostering self-awareness without criticism.

Theme: Motivation
- January 30: "Obstacles are invitations to innovate and grow."
- Note: View obstacles as opportunities to innovate and grow, turning challenges into catalysts for development.

Theme: Personal Growth
- January 31: "I let go of what no longer serves me."
- Note: Release old habits or beliefs that hinder your growth, making room for new, beneficial changes.

This sequence of daily affirmations for January is designed to provide a variety of perspectives and themes, ensuring that each day offers fresh inspiration and guidance. The aim is to support and encourage mindfulness, motivation, personal growth, and a sense of success through thoughtful and meaningful affirmations.

February - Self-Love and Acceptance: Highlighting the importance of loving oneself, embracing individuality, and cultivating self-compassion.

Theme: Success
   - February 1: "I create my own path to success."
   - Note: Believe in your ability to forge your own unique path to achieving your goals.

Theme: Mindfulness
   - February 2: "Every breath I take brings me closer to inner peace."
   - Note: Use your breath as a tool to cultivate inner peace, anchoring yourself in the present moment.

Theme: Motivation
   - February 3: "I am energized by the possibilities of today."
   - Note: Approach the day with enthusiasm, focusing on the potential it holds.

Theme: Personal Growth
   - February 4: "I grow stronger from the challenges I face."
   - Note: Embrace challenges as opportunities to strengthen your character and abilities.

Theme: Success
   - February 5: "My efforts are being supported by the universe; my dreams manifest into reality before my eyes."
   - Note: Trust that your efforts are aligned with the greater forces at play, bringing your dreams to fruition.

Theme: Mindfulness

- February 6: "I am mindful of my impact on the world around me."

- Note: Be conscious of how your actions and presence affect the world and people around you.

Theme: Motivation

- February 7: "I tackle my to-do list with energy and enthusiasm."

- Note: Approach your tasks with a positive mindset, turning even routine activities into opportunities for fulfillment.

Theme: Personal Growth

- February 8: "Every day, I learn something new about myself."

- Note: Stay open to self-discovery, understanding that personal growth often comes from unexpected insights.

Theme: Success

- February 9: "I am deserving of abundance and prosperity."

- Note: Affirm your worthiness to receive abundance and success in all its forms.

Theme: Mindfulness

- February 10: "I treat myself with kindness and respect."

- Note: Practice self-compassion, recognizing that how you treat yourself sets the tone for your overall well-being.

Theme: Motivation

- February 11: "I am unstoppable in pursuing my goals."

- Note: Embrace a sense of unstoppable drive and determination in working towards your aspirations.

Theme: Personal Growth

- February 12: "I gracefully accept and learn from my mistakes."
- Note: See mistakes as valuable learning opportunities and embrace them without harsh judgment.

Theme: Success

- February 13: "Every step I take is leading me to greater success."
- Note: Recognize that each action, no matter how small, is a progressive step towards achieving greater success.

Theme: Mindfulness

- February 14: "I am centered and calm in the midst of life's storms."
- Note: Cultivate a sense of inner calm that remains unshaken, even in turbulent times.

Theme: Motivation

- February 15: "I find motivation in the challenges I face."
- Note: Convert challenges into sources of motivation, driving you to overcome and succeed.

Theme: Personal Growth

- February 16: "I am evolving into the best version of myself."
- Note: Acknowledge and appreciate your ongoing journey of self-evolution and improvement.

Theme: Success

- February 17: "Success and joy are abundant in my life."
- Note: Affirm the abundance of success and joy in your life, attracting more of the same.

Theme: Mindfulness
- February 18: "I am aware of the beauty and wonder that surrounds me."
- Note: Take the time to notice and appreciate the beauty in the world around you, enhancing your sense of mindfulness.

Theme: Motivation
- February 19: "I embrace today with renewed energy and determination."
- Note: Start your day with a fresh burst of energy and a resolved spirit to tackle your tasks.

Theme: Personal Growth
- February 20: "I am constantly evolving and embracing new heights."
- Note: Acknowledge your continuous growth and the journey to reaching new heights in your personal development.

Theme: Success
- February 21: "My actions today are laying the foundation for my future success."
- Note: Recognize that your daily actions are crucial building blocks for your future achievements.

Theme: Mindfulness
- February 22: "I find clarity and peace in my quiet moments."
- Note: Cherish the quiet moments, as they bring clarity and

peace essential for mindfulness.

Theme: Motivation

- February 23: "I am driven by my passion to achieve extraordinary things."
- Note: Let your passion be the driving force that propels you towards accomplishing remarkable feats.

Theme: Personal Growth

- February 24: "I welcome growth and the changes it brings."
- Note: Embrace the changes that come with growth, understanding they are part of your evolution.

Theme: Success

- February 25: "I am worthy of achieving my greatest dreams."
- Note: Affirm your worthiness and capability to realize your biggest dreams and aspirations.

Theme: Mindfulness

- February 26: "In each moment, I find opportunities to be mindful."
- Note: Look for opportunities in every moment to practice mindfulness, enhancing your awareness and presence.

Theme: Motivation

- February 27: "My motivation is unbreakable; no obstacle can deter my path."
- Note: Strengthen your resolve, affirming that no challenge is too great to deter you from your goals.

Theme: Personal Growth
  - February 28: "Each day, I am better than I was yesterday."
  - Note: Recognize and appreciate your daily progress and continuous improvement.

Theme: Success
  -Leap Year Special
  - February 29: "Every extra day is a precious gift for more success."_
  - Note: In a leap year, view February 29th as a bonus opportunity to advance towards your goals and celebrate the extra time granted for success.

These affirmations provide a guide for each day, offering insights and encouragement relevant to the themes of mindfulness, motivation, personal growth, and success. The inclusion of February 29th in leap years ensures that every day of the year is an opportunity for reflection, growth, and positive affirmation.

March - Resilience and Strength: Concentrating on building inner strength, overcoming challenges, and fostering resilience in the face of adversity.

Theme: Mindfulness
- March 1: "I am in tune with the natural rhythm of life."
- Note: Align yourself with life's natural flow, finding harmony in its rhythm.

Theme: Motivation
- March 2: "I have the power to create positive change in my life."
- Note: Empower yourself with the belief that you are the architect of your own life's positive transformations.

Theme: Personal Growth
- March 3: "I am open to new ideas and different perspectives."
- Note: Embrace openness, allowing new ideas and perspectives to broaden your understanding and personal growth.

Theme: Success
- March 4: "I celebrate each milestone on my journey to success."
- Note: Take time to acknowledge and celebrate every small victory and milestone on your path to success.

Theme: Mindfulness
- March 5: "I appreciate the beauty in every day."
- Note: Cultivate an attitude of gratitude and appreciation for the everyday beauty surrounding you.

Theme: Motivation

- March 6: "My dreams are within reach, and I am motivated to achieve them."
- Note: Keep your dreams in focus and let this vision motivate your daily actions and decisions.

Theme: Personal Growth

- March 7: "I am a lifelong learner, constantly acquiring new knowledge and skills."
- Note: Embrace the identity of a lifelong learner, always open to acquiring new knowledge and skills.

Theme: Success

- March 8: "I attract success by being authentic and true to myself."
- Note: Believe in the power of authenticity as a key to attracting success in all areas of life.

Theme: Mindfulness

- March 9: "I find serenity in my ability to be patient."
- Note: Embrace patience as a path to inner peace and mindfulness.

Theme: Motivation

- March 10: "My enthusiasm is the engine that drives my success."
- Note: Use your natural enthusiasm as a powerful force to propel you towards your goals.

Theme: Personal Growth

- March 11: "I am not afraid to step out of my comfort zone."

- Note: Encourage yourself to embrace new challenges as opportunities for personal growth.

Theme: Success
- March 12: "I am confident in my ability to overcome obstacles."
- Note: Affirm your confidence in facing and overcoming challenges, seeing them as stepping stones to success.

Theme: Mindfulness
- March 13: "I am mindful in my interactions with others."
- Note: Practice being present and attentive in your interactions, enhancing your relationships and understanding of others.

Theme: Motivation
- March 14: "I am motivated by my desire to make a positive impact."
- Note: Let your desire to contribute positively to the world be a source of daily motivation.

Theme: Personal Growth
- March 15: "I embrace the lessons that life teaches me."
- Note: See life's experiences as valuable lessons that contribute to your personal growth and wisdom.

Theme: Success
- March 16: "I am a magnet for success in all its forms."
- Note: Cultivate the belief that you naturally attract success in its many forms.

Theme: Mindfulness

- March 17: "Today, I embrace the art of being still and listening."
- Note: Practice stillness, finding wisdom and insight in the quiet moments.

Theme: Motivation

- March 18: "My dreams are my motivation to move forward."
- Note: Keep your dreams at the forefront as a constant source of motivation.

Theme: Personal Growth

- March 19: "Every experience enriches my journey."
- Note: View every experience, good or bad, as an enriching part of your personal journey.

Theme: Success

- March 20: "I am the architect of my success; I build its foundation daily."
- Note: Recognize your role in creating your success, one day at a time.

Theme: Mindfulness

- March 21: "I find joy in the simplicity of living mindfully."
- Note: Discover joy in the simple act of living with mindfulness and awareness.

Theme: Motivation

- March 22: "My passion is the fuel for my perseverance."
- Note: Let your passion be the driving force that keeps you persevering through challenges.

Theme: Personal Growth

- March 23: "I am committed to evolving positively with each passing day."
- Note: Dedicate yourself to positive evolution, embracing change and growth every day.

Theme: Success

- March 24: "Success is my natural state; I welcome it in abundance."
- Note: Affirm your belief in your natural ability to succeed and attract abundance.

Theme: Mindfulness

- March 25: "I embrace the present with gratitude and openness."
- Note: Practice gratitude for the present moment, embracing it with an open heart and mind.

Theme: Motivation

- March 26: "I am inspired by my journey and excited for the future."
- Note: Draw inspiration from your personal journey and look forward to the future with excitement and optimism.

Theme: Personal Growth

- March 27: "I welcome growth and the new perspectives it brings."
- Note: Embrace the growth process and the fresh perspectives it introduces to your life.

Theme: Success

- March 28: "My actions today are planting seeds for tomorrow's success."
- Note: Acknowledge that your current actions are laying the groundwork for future success.

Theme: Mindfulness
- March 29: "I find clarity and calmness in my mindful moments."
- Note: In moments of mindfulness, seek clarity and calmness as a path to inner peace.

Theme: Motivation
- March 30: "I possess an unyielding drive to achieve my goals."
- Note: Affirm the strength of your determination and drive in achieving your objectives.

Theme: Personal Growth
- March 31: "Each day is an opportunity to learn and grow stronger."
- Note: View each day as a valuable chance for learning and strengthening your character.

This concludes the affirmations for March, each one tailored to inspire and guide you through the themes of mindfulness, motivation, personal growth, and success. These affirmations are designed to provide daily encouragement, helping you to maintain a positive outlook and continually strive for personal betterment.

April - Growth and Renewal: Reflecting the spirit of spring, this month emphasizes personal growth, learning from experiences, and embracing change.

Theme: Success
   - April 1: "I embrace new opportunities with confidence and courage."
   - Note: Approach new opportunities with a mindset of confidence and the courage to take them on.

Theme: Mindfulness
   - April 2: "I am fully present in every interaction today."
   - Note: Make a conscious effort to be fully present and engaged in each interaction throughout your day.

Theme: Motivation
   - April 3: "My determination is unwavering, and my spirit is unstoppable."
   - Note: Affirm the strength of your determination and the resilience of your spirit in the face of challenges.

Theme: Personal Growth
   - April 4: "I embrace change as it fosters my personal development."
   - Note: View change as a positive force, an opportunity for learning and personal evolution.

Theme: Success
   - April 5: "Every goal I set is clear, achievable, and within reach."

- Note: Set clear and attainable goals, believing in your ability to achieve them.

Theme: Mindfulness
- April 6: "I find peace in letting go of what I cannot control."
- Note: Cultivate peace of mind by focusing on what you can control and releasing worries about what you cannot.

Theme: Motivation
- April 7: "I am fueled by the progress I make each day."
- Note: Let the progress you make, no matter how small, be a source of daily motivation.

Theme: Personal Growth
- April 8: "I continuously seek to expand my horizons and understanding."
- Note: Be proactive in seeking new experiences and knowledge that broaden your perspective.

Theme: Success
- April 9: "I attract success by working hard and believing in my abilities."
- Note: Hard work combined with self-belief is a powerful recipe for attracting success.

Theme: Mindfulness
- April 10: "Today, I am mindful of my health and well-being."
- Note: Pay attention to your physical and mental health, nurturing them as a priority.

Theme: Motivation

- April 11: "My actions today are shaping my future."

- Note: Recognize that your present actions have a significant impact on shaping your future.

Theme: Personal Growth

- April 12: "I embrace my journey, with its ups and downs, as a path to growth."

- Note: Acknowledge that the highs and lows are all part of the journey toward personal growth.

Theme: Success

- April 13: "I am a success magnet, attracting opportunities and achievements."

- Note: Cultivate the mindset that you naturally attract success and opportunities.

Theme: Mindfulness

- April 14: "In stillness, I find wisdom and understanding."

- Note: Use moments of stillness to tap into deeper wisdom and understanding.

Theme: Motivation

- April 15: "Every obstacle I overcome makes me stronger."

- Note: View each obstacle as a chance to grow stronger and more resilient.

Theme: Personal Growth

- April 16: "I am committed to learning from my experiences."

- Note: Approach every experience as a learning opportunity, growing in wisdom with each one.

Theme: Success
 - April 17: "Success is not just about achievement but also about the journey."
 - Note: Remember that the path to success is as important as the achievements themselves.

Theme: Mindfulness
 - April 18: "I live each day with intention and purpose."
 - Note: Approach each day with clear intentions, living purposefully and mindfully.

Theme: Motivation
 - April 19: "I have the power within me to create the life I desire."
 - Note: Believe in your inner power to create and shape the life you want.

Theme: Personal Growth
 - April 20: "I am adaptable and open to new ways of thinking."
 - Note: Embrace adaptability and openness as key qualities for personal growth and development.

Continuing in this pattern, the affirmations for the rest of April focus on the themes of success, mindfulness, motivation, and personal growth. Each day offers a new perspective or insight to guide and encourage you in your daily life, contributing to a mindset of positivity and self-improvement.

Theme: Success

- April 21: "I celebrate every small victory on my path to success."
- Note: Recognize and celebrate each small achievement, as they cumulatively lead to great success.

Theme: Mindfulness
- April 22: "I am connected with the beauty of the present moment."
- Note: Take time to connect with and appreciate the beauty and uniqueness of the present moment.

Theme: Motivation
- April 23: "My motivation is renewed each morning; I greet the day with energy."
- Note: Start each day with a renewed sense of motivation and energy, greeting the day with enthusiasm.

Theme: Personal Growth
- April 24: "I am continuously growing and transforming in positive ways."
- Note: Acknowledge your ongoing transformation and growth, embracing the positive changes within you.

Theme: Success
- April 25: "I define my own success and work towards it every day."
- Note: Personalize your definition of success and diligently work towards achieving it.

Theme: Mindfulness
- April 26: "I am aware of my thoughts and control their

impact on my life."

- Note: Practice awareness of your thoughts and their influence on your life, choosing positivity and constructive thinking.

Theme: Motivation
- April 27: "I am inspired by the challenges I face; they bring out my best."
- Note: Let challenges be a source of inspiration, pushing you to bring out your best self.

Theme: Personal Growth
- April 28: "My journey is unique, and I embrace it with confidence."
- Note: Celebrate the uniqueness of your personal journey, embracing it with confidence and self-assurance.

Theme: Success
- April 29: "I trust my intuition and experience to lead me to success."
- Note: Trust in your intuition and past experiences as valuable guides to achieving success.

Theme: Mindfulness
- April 30: "I end each day with gratitude for its lessons and experiences."
- Note: Conclude each day with gratitude, appreciating the lessons and experiences it brought.

This pattern of daily affirmations for April, centered around success, mindfulness, motivation, and personal growth, is designed to provide daily support and guidance. Each affirmation helps to cultivate a mindset that is conducive to personal development and achieving one's goals.

May - Mindfulness and Presence: Focusing on living in the moment, practicing mindfulness, and appreciating the present.

Theme: Motivation
  - May 1: "I am fueled by the energy of spring to renew my efforts towards my goals."
  - Note: Embrace the renewing energy of spring to reinvigorate your efforts and focus on your goals.

Theme: Personal Growth
  - May 2: "I welcome new perspectives and ideas that challenge and grow me."
  - Note: Be open to new ideas and viewpoints; they are opportunities for personal expansion and growth.

Theme: Success
  - May 3: "I celebrate the progress I've made, knowing each step forward is a success."
  - Note: Acknowledge and celebrate your progress, understanding that every step forward is a part of your success story.

Theme: Mindfulness
  - May 4: "I am mindful of my impact on the environment and strive to make positive contributions."
  - Note: Be conscious of your environmental impact and seek

ways to contribute positively to the world around you.

Theme: Motivation
- May 5: "Challenges strengthen my resolve and sharpen my skills."
- Note: View challenges as opportunities to strengthen your resolve and enhance your abilities.

Theme: Personal Growth
- May 6: "I am constantly evolving, embracing change as a path to self-improvement."
- Note: Recognize that constant evolution and embracing change are key to your journey of self-improvement.

Theme: Success
- May 7: "My efforts create a ripple effect of success in various aspects of my life."
- Note: Understand that your efforts can create a positive impact across different areas of your life.

Theme: Mindfulness
- May 8: "I cherish each moment and find the extraordinary in the ordinary."
- Note: Make an effort to find joy and extraordinariness in everyday moments.

Theme: Motivation
- May 9: "I am unstoppable in my pursuit of excellence."
- Note: Affirm your unwavering commitment to pursue excellence in all that you do.

Theme: Personal Growth

- May 10: "I am a blend of strength and compassion, constantly growing in balance."

- Note: Recognize and cultivate a balance of strength and compassion within yourself as part of your growth.

Theme: Success

- May 11: "I am deserving of abundance and prosperity in all forms."

- Note: Acknowledge your worthiness of success and abundance in every area of your life.

Theme: Mindfulness

- May 12: "I am in harmony with the rhythm of my day, finding balance in all activities."

- Note: Strive for balance throughout your day, finding harmony in both busy moments and times of rest.

Theme: Motivation

- May 13: "I turn obstacles into opportunities for growth and advancement."

- Note: View each obstacle as a chance to grow stronger and to advance in your personal and professional life.

Theme: Personal Growth

- May 14: "I trust in my journey, knowing each step contributes to my growth."

- Note: Have faith in your personal journey, understanding that every experience contributes to your overall growth.

Theme: Success

- May 15: "I am capable of achieving great things when I set my mind to them."
- Note: Embrace your ability to achieve remarkable things through determination and focus.

Theme: Mindfulness
- May 16: "Today, I choose to respond with compassion and understanding."
- Note: Make a conscious decision to approach situations with compassion and empathy.

Theme: Motivation
- May 17: "My passion is a powerful force that drives me forward."
- Note: Let your passion be the driving force that propels you towards achieving your goals.

Theme: Personal Growth
- May 18: "I am open to new experiences, knowing they shape and enrich my character."
- Note: Embrace new experiences, as they are opportunities to shape and enrich your character and worldview.

Theme: Success
- May 19: "Every effort I put forth manifests success in various aspects of my life."
- Note: Recognize that your efforts contribute to success in multiple facets of your life.

Theme: Mindfulness
- May 20: "I find joy and peace in the present moment."

- Note: Focus on experiencing joy and peace in the present, embracing the now fully.

Theme: Motivation
- May 21: "I am dedicated to turning my dreams into reality."
- Note: Foster a sense of dedication towards making your dreams a tangible reality.

Theme: Personal Growth
- May 22: "I continuously seek to expand my boundaries and step beyond them."
- Note: Embrace the idea of constantly pushing and expanding your limits for personal growth.

Theme: Success
- May 23: "Success is a journey I walk with confidence and determination."
- Note: Approach your path to success with confidence and a strong determination to overcome challenges.

Theme: Mindfulness
- May 24: "I am attentive to my needs and nourish myself with kindness and care."
- Note: Be mindful of your personal needs and treat yourself with kindness and care.

Theme: Motivation
- May 25: "Each day, I am motivated by a strong sense of purpose."
- Note: Let a strong sense of purpose fuel your daily motivation.

Theme: Personal Growth

- May 26: "I embrace learning from both successes and failures."
- Note: Acknowledge that both successes and failures offer valuable learning opportunities.

Theme: Success

- May 27: "I create opportunities for success through my actions and mindset."
- Note: Believe in your ability to create opportunities for success actively.

Theme: Mindfulness

- May 28: "Today, I choose to live with gratitude and grace."
- Note: Make a conscious choice to live with gratitude, appreciating the blessings in your life.

Theme: Motivation

- May 29: "I am resilient and bounce back stronger from setbacks."
- Note: Affirm your resilience and ability to recover strongly from any setbacks.

Theme: Personal Growth

- May 30: "I am committed to self-improvement and constantly seek to better myself."
- Note: Dedicate yourself to continuous self-improvement and personal development.

Theme: Success

- May 31: "My actions are aligned with my vision of success."

- Note: Ensure your actions consistently align with your vision and goals for success.

The affirmations for the end of May continue to provide motivation, encourage personal growth, inspire success, and promote mindfulness. Each one is crafted to help you maintain focus on your goals while cultivating a positive and balanced approach to everyday life.

June - Joy and Gratitude: Centering on finding joy in everyday life, expressing gratitude, and celebrating small victories.

Theme: Mindfulness
- June 1: "I find peace in nature and connect with its calming energy."
- Note: Spend time in nature to reconnect with its tranquil and rejuvenating energy.

Theme: Motivation
- June 2: "My aspirations are the fuel for my actions today."
- Note: Let your aspirations drive your actions, turning dreams into reality.

Theme: Personal Growth
- June 3: "I am open to different perspectives and learn from everyone I meet."
- Note: Embrace openness to learn from diverse perspectives and experiences.

Theme: Success

- June 4: "I recognize and seize opportunities for growth and success."
- Note: Be alert to opportunities that come your way and seize them with confidence.

Theme: Mindfulness

- June 5: "I am mindful of my words and actions and their impact on others."
- Note: Practice mindfulness in your communication and actions, considering their effects on those around you.

Theme: Motivation

- June 6: "I rise above challenges and use them as stepping stones."
- Note: View challenges as opportunities to rise higher and advance your goals.

Theme: Personal Growth

- June 7: "I continuously strive to understand myself better."
- Note: Make self-understanding a priority, as it's key to personal growth and fulfillment.

Theme: Success

- June 8: "I am a creator of success; it starts with my mindset and actions."
- Note: Affirm that success begins with your mindset and actions, and you are its creator.

Theme: Mindfulness

- June 9: "I appreciate the present for its unique gifts and lessons."

- Note: Value the present moment for the unique opportunities and lessons it offers.

Theme: Motivation

- June 10: "My motivation is grounded in my desire to make a positive difference."

- Note: Base your motivation on the desire to contribute positively to your surroundings and the world.

Theme: Personal Growth

- June 11: "Every experience, good or bad, is a valuable lesson for my growth."

- Note: Embrace every experience as a learning opportunity, contributing to your growth.

Theme: Success

- June 12: "My journey towards success is filled with perseverance and resilience."

- Note: Acknowledge the role of perseverance and resilience in navigating the path to success.

Theme: Mindfulness

- June 13: "I am in harmony with my thoughts and emotions."

- Note: Strive for a balance between your thoughts and emotions, cultivating inner harmony.

Theme: Motivation

- June 14: "I am inspired by the journey, not just the destination."

- Note: Find motivation in the journey towards your goals,

not just in the achievement of the goals themselves.

Theme: Personal Growth

- June 15: "I am open to change, for it is the catalyst for personal transformation."
- Note: Embrace change as a necessary and positive force for personal transformation.

Theme: Success

- June 16: "I celebrate my accomplishments, no matter how small."
- Note: Take time to celebrate all of your accomplishments, as each one is significant.

Theme: Mindfulness

- June 17: "I find strength and peace in my moments of solitude."
- Note: Value your moments of solitude as opportunities for strength and peace.

Theme: Motivation

- June 18: "Every challenge is a chance to showcase my strength and creativity."
- Note: Approach challenges as opportunities to demonstrate your strength and creativity.

Theme: Personal Growth

- June 19: "I am constantly evolving into a more insightful and compassionate person."
- Note: Recognize and appreciate your continuous evolution towards greater insight and compassion.

Theme: Success
- June 20: "Success to me means living a life true to my values and beliefs."
- Note: Define success on your own terms, aligning it with your values and beliefs.

Theme: Mindfulness
- June 21: "I am attentive to the beauty and richness of the present moment."
- Note: Cultivate attentiveness to the beauty and richness of the here and now.

Theme: Motivation
- June 22: "I draw motivation from my past achievements and future aspirations."
- Note: Use your past successes and future goals as sources of motivation.

Theme: Personal Growth
- June 23: "Every day, I strive to expand my understanding and deepen my knowledge."
- Note: Commit to expanding your understanding and deepening your knowledge every day.

Theme: Success
- June 24: "I am confident in my journey towards achieving my dreams."
- Note: Maintain confidence in your journey towards realizing your dreams.

Theme: Mindfulness

- June 25: "I consciously create moments of stillness in my busy day."
- Note: Intentionally incorporate moments of stillness into your day to reconnect with yourself.

Theme: Motivation

- June 26: "My goals are clear, and my path is set. I am ready to move forward."
- Note: Affirm the clarity of your goals and your readiness to advance towards them.

Theme: Personal Growth

- June 27: "I embrace my unique qualities and use them as strengths."
- Note: Recognize and utilize your unique qualities as strengths in your

   personal and professional life.

Theme: Success

- June 28: "I am a beacon of success and positivity in my community."
- Note: See yourself as a source of success and positivity, influencing your community in a constructive manner.

Theme: Mindfulness

- June 29: "I approach my challenges with a calm and mindful attitude."
- Note: Use mindfulness to face challenges with calmness, helping you make thoughtful and effective decisions.

Theme: Motivation

- June 30: "My passion ignites my drive to excel in all that I undertake."
- Note: Let your passion be the spark that drives you to excel and achieve in every endeavor.

This completes the affirmations for June, each one crafted to inspire and guide you through the themes of mindfulness, motivation, personal growth, and success. These daily affirmations are designed to provide a source of strength, inspiration, and reflection, helping you to maintain a positive outlook and continually strive for personal betterment.

July - Freedom and Independence: Emphasizing personal freedom, self-reliance, and the courage to be true to oneself.

Theme: Personal Growth
- July 1: "I embrace the journey of self-discovery and cherish each discovery along the way."
- Note: Value your journey of self-discovery, understanding that each realization contributes to your growth.

Theme: Success
- July 2: "I am an architect of my future, building it with purpose and intention."
- Note: Recognize your role in shaping your future through purposeful actions and intentions.

Theme: Mindfulness

- July 3: "Today, I choose to focus on what truly matters and let go of trivial worries."
- Note: Prioritize your focus on significant matters and release concerns over trivialities.

Theme: Motivation
- July 4: "My dreams are the blueprint for my actions today."
- Note: Let your dreams guide your actions, using them as a blueprint for today's endeavors.

Theme: Personal Growth
- July 5: "I am open to learning from both triumphs and setbacks."
- Note: Embrace learning from all experiences, whether they are triumphs or setbacks, as both contribute to your wisdom.

Theme: Success
- July 6: "Success for me is about balancing happiness, health, and achievement."
- Note: Define success as a balance between your happiness, health, and accomplishments.

Theme: Mindfulness
- July 7: "I practice gratitude daily, recognizing the abundance in my life."
- Note: Cultivate a daily practice of gratitude to recognize and appreciate the abundance surrounding you.

Theme: Motivation
- July 8: "I am energized by challenges and see them as opportunities to excel."

- Note: View challenges as opportunities that energize you and provide a chance to excel.

Theme: Personal Growth
- July 9: "I continually seek to break my own limits and expand my horizons."
- Note: Aim to constantly break through your own limits and expand your horizons for continual personal growth.

Theme: Success
- July 10: "I create success by bringing my best self to every situation."
- Note: Believe that bringing your best self to every situation is a key to creating success.

Theme: Mindfulness
- July 11: "I find joy and contentment in the simplicity of life."
- Note: Appreciate the simple pleasures of life, finding joy and contentment in the everyday.

Theme: Motivation
- July 12: "I am driven by a deep sense of purpose and commitment to my goals."
- Note: Let a strong sense of purpose and commitment to your goals be the driving force behind your actions.

Theme: Personal Growth
- July 13: "I am constantly adapting and growing in the face of change."
- Note: Embrace adaptability as a key strength, allowing you to grow and thrive amidst change.

Theme: Success

- July 14: "I am a trailblazer, confidently paving my path to success."
- Note: Affirm your role as a trailblazer, confidently creating your own path to success.

Theme: Mindfulness

- July 15: "I am present in my interactions, fully engaging with those around me."
- Note: Practice being fully present and engaged in your interactions, enhancing your connections with others.

Theme: Motivation

- July 16: "My enthusiasm for life is a source of energy for achieving my dreams."
- Note: Draw upon your enthusiasm for life as a powerful source of energy for realizing your dreams.

Theme: Personal Growth

- July 17: "I welcome constructive feedback as a tool for personal and professional growth."
- Note: View constructive feedback as a valuable tool for your personal and professional development.

Theme: Success

- July 18: "I am competent, skilled, and prepared for the opportunities that come my way."
- Note: Affirm your competence, skills, and preparedness for seizing opportunities.

Theme: Mindfulness

- July 19: "Each day, I take time to reflect and find peace within myself."
- Note: Dedicate time each day for self-reflection, finding inner peace and clarity.

Theme: Motivation
- July 20: "I am unstoppable in my journey towards achieving my goals."
- Note: Embrace an unstoppable attitude in your journey toward achieving your goals.

Theme: Personal Growth
- July 21: "I embrace my flaws as part of my unique journey of growth."
- Note: Recognize and accept your flaws as integral parts of your unique growth journey.

Theme: Success
- July 22: "I am worthy of the success I aspire to and work towards it with dedication."
- Note: Affirm your worthiness of success and approach your aspirations with unwavering dedication.

Theme: Mindfulness
- July 23: "In every experience, I seek to be fully aware and engaged."
- Note: Strive to be fully aware and actively engaged in every experience you encounter.

Theme: Motivation
- July 24: "I choose to rise above doubts and keep my focus

on my goals."

- Note: Rise above any doubts, keeping your focus steadfast on your goals.

Theme: Personal Growth

- July 25: "I continuously strive to unlock new levels of my potential."
- Note: Commit to unlocking and exploring new levels of your potential continuously.

Theme: Success

- July 26: "I am a beacon of positivity, attracting success in all areas of my life."
- Note: Cultivate a positive demeanor, attracting success in every aspect of your life.

Theme: Mindfulness

- July 27: "I am in tune with the needs of my body and mind, nurturing them with care."
- Note: Pay attention to and care for the needs of both your body and mind.

Theme: Motivation

- July 28: "I have the power and determination to turn challenges into triumphs."
- Note: Believe in your power and determination to transform challenges into victories.

Theme: Personal Growth

- July 29: "I welcome diverse experiences as opportunities to expand my worldview."

- Note: Open yourself to diverse experiences, seeing them as chances to broaden your perspective.

Theme: Success
- July 30: "My journey to success is marked by perseverance and resilience."
- Note: Recognize perseverance and resilience as key markers on your journey to success.

Theme: Mindfulness
- July 31: "I end each day with gratitude, reflecting on the lessons and blessings."
- Note: Conclude each day with a sense of gratitude, reflecting on the day's lessons and blessings.

These affirmations for July encourage a mindset that fosters personal growth, motivation, mindfulness, and a successful approach to life's challenges and opportunities.

August - Reflection and Introspection: Dedicated to self-reflection, understanding personal desires, and introspection.

Theme: Motivation

- August 1: "I am motivated by my past achievements and excited for future accomplishments."
- Note: Use your past achievements as fuel for future goals, keeping your motivation high.

Theme: Personal Growth

- August 2: "I am constantly evolving, embracing each change as a part of my growth."
- Note: View each change in your life as an essential part of your continuous evolution and growth.

Theme: Success

- August 3: "Success is a reflection of my hard work and dedication."
- Note: Recognize that your success is a direct result of your hard work and dedication.

Theme: Mindfulness

- August 4: "I find joy and peace in the now, living each moment to its fullest."
- Note: Embrace the present moment, finding joy and peace in the here and now.

Theme: Motivation

- August 5: "My actions are purposeful and lead me closer to my goals."

- Note: Ensure that your actions are intentional and contribute to bringing you closer to your goals.

Theme: Personal Growth

- August 6: "I am open to new challenges; they are opportunities for growth."

- Note: Approach new challenges with openness, seeing them as valuable opportunities for personal growth.

Theme: Success

- August 7: "I believe in my ability to overcome any obstacle and succeed."

- Note: Have faith in your ability to overcome challenges and achieve success.

Theme: Mindfulness

- August 8: "I practice patience and understanding in all aspects of my life."

- Note: Cultivate patience and understanding, applying them to all areas of your life.

Theme: Motivation

- August 9: "I am driven by a passion for learning and growing."

- Note: Let your passion for learning and self-improvement be a key driver in your life.

Theme: Personal Growth

- August 10: "I embrace my unique journey, learning from each step along the way."

- Note: Value your unique life journey and the lessons it brings at every step.

Theme: Success
- August 11: "I am the master of my destiny, creating success with my choices and actions."
- Note: Affirm your role in shaping your future and success through deliberate choices and actions.

Theme: Mindfulness
- August 12: "I cherish the present, finding beauty in the simplicity of life."
- Note: Focus on the present moment, appreciating the simple beauties of everyday life.

Theme: Motivation
- August 13: "I am resilient, facing each day with strength and determination."
- Note: Embrace each day with resilience, strength, and determination, no matter the challenges.

Theme: Personal Growth
- August 14: "I am a lifelong learner, continuously expanding my understanding of the world."
- Note: Commit to lifelong learning, continuously broadening your perspective and understanding.

Theme: Success
- August 15: "Success is my journey, marked by personal growth and achievements."
- Note: View your journey to success as a path marked by

continuous personal growth and achievements.

Theme: Mindfulness
- August 16: "I am in tune with my inner self, listening to its wisdom and guidance."
- Note: Cultivate a connection with your inner self, listening to its wisdom and guidance for clarity.

Theme: Motivation
- August 17: "Each challenge I overcome fuels my motivation to achieve more."
- Note: Use the challenges you overcome as fuel to drive your motivation for further achievements.

Theme: Personal Growth
- August 18: "I embrace the unknown, seeing it as a journey of discovery and opportunity."
- Note: Approach the unknown with a sense of discovery, seeing it as a journey filled with opportunities.

Theme: Success
- August 19: "I attract success by aligning my actions with my goals."
- Note: Align your daily actions with your goals to naturally attract success.

Theme: Mindfulness
- August 20: "I find balance in my life by giving attention to my mind, body, and spirit."
- Note: Strive for balance in life by nurturing your mind, body, and spirit equally.

Theme: Motivation

- August 21: "My dreams are the blueprints of my motivation, guiding me forward."

- Note: Let your dreams be the blueprints that guide your daily motivation.

Theme: Personal Growth

- August 22: "I welcome growth from every experience, building wisdom and strength."

- Note: Embrace growth from all experiences, as they build your wisdom and inner strength.

Theme: Success

- August 23: "I celebrate my small victories, as they lead to great achievements."

- Note: Acknowledge and celebrate your small victories, as they are essential steps towards larger achievements.

Theme: Mindfulness

- August 24: "I am mindful of my impact on others and the world, striving to make positive contributions."

- Note: Be conscious of your impact and strive to contribute positively to others and the world.

Theme: Motivation

- August 25: "I am unstoppable, turning barriers into bridges towards my goals."

- Note: View barriers as opportunities to build bridges that lead to your goals.

Theme: Personal Growth

- August 26: "I am adaptable, embracing change as a path to new possibilities."
- Note: Embrace adaptability and view change as an open door to new possibilities and experiences.

Theme: Success
- August 27: "My hard work and dedication are the cornerstones of my success."
- Note: Recognize that your hard work and dedication are fundamental to achieving success.

Theme: Mindfulness
- August 28: "I savor each moment, finding richness in life's experiences."
- Note: Take time to savor each moment, appreciating the richness of life's diverse experiences.

Theme: Motivation
- August 29: "Every day, I move closer to my dreams with unwavering focus and effort."
- Note: Keep moving towards your dreams each day with focus and dedicated effort.

Theme: Personal Growth
- August 30: "I reflect on my experiences, learning valuable lessons for the future."
- Note: Reflect on your experiences, extracting valuable lessons to guide your future decisions.

Theme: Success
- August 31: "I am successful in my personal and professional

endeavors, achieving harmony and fulfillment."

- Note: Aim for success in both personal and professional areas of your life, achieving a harmonious and fulfilling existence.

These affirmations for August are designed to provide daily inspiration and guidance, focusing on achieving success, practicing mindfulness, staying motivated, and embracing personal growth. Each affirmation encourages a positive mindset and proactive approach to life's challenges and opportunities.

September - Focus and Clarity: Concentrating on setting clear goals, staying focused, and prioritizing important tasks as the year progresses.

Theme: Mindfulness
- September 1: "I embrace the change of seasons with a mindful appreciation of the past and optimism for the future."
- Note: Use the transition of seasons as a time to reflect mindfully on the past and look forward to the future with optimism.

Theme: Motivation
- September 2: "I am energized by my goals and motivated by the progress I make each day."
- Note: Draw energy from your goals and the daily progress you make towards achieving them.

Theme: Personal Growth
- September 3: "I welcome new experiences as opportunities

for learning and self-discovery."

- Note: View new experiences as chances to learn more about yourself and the world around you.

Theme: Success

- September 4: "My efforts and determination today lay the foundation for my future success."

- Note: Recognize that your current efforts and determination are key building blocks for your future success.

Theme: Mindfulness

- September 5: "I find peace in the quiet moments of the day, recharging my mind and spirit."

- Note: Use quiet moments to find peace and recharge, giving attention to your mental and spiritual well-being.

Theme: Motivation

- September 6: "I confront challenges with courage and confidence, turning them into opportunities for growth."

- Note: Face challenges with courage, transforming them into valuable opportunities for personal growth.

Theme: Personal Growth

- September 7: "I am a better version of myself with each passing day, embracing both strengths and weaknesses."

- Note: Acknowledge and embrace your continuous improvement, including both your strengths and areas for growth.

Theme: Success

- September 8: "I am successful in maintaining a balance between work, life, and personal well-being."

- Note: Aim for success in balancing your professional responsibilities, personal life, and overall well-being.

Theme: Mindfulness
- September 9: "I appreciate the beauty and lessons of nature, finding mindfulness in its rhythms."
- Note: Connect with nature, appreciating its beauty and the mindfulness it inspires through its natural rhythms.

Theme: Motivation
- September 10: "My passion is the driving force that propels me forward towards my aspirations."
- Note: Let your passion be the driving force that propels you towards your aspirations and goals.

Theme: Personal Growth
- September 11: "I learn and grow from every situation, embracing both challenges and triumphs."
- Note: See every situation, whether challenging or triumphant, as an opportunity for learning and growth.

Theme: Success
- September 12: "I am a magnet for success, attracting opportunities and achievements."
- Note: Cultivate the belief that you naturally attract success and opportunities in your life.

Theme: Mindfulness
- September 13: "I am conscious of my thoughts and actions, ensuring they align with my true self."
- Note: Be mindful of your thoughts and actions, making sure

they reflect your authentic self.

Theme: Motivation
   - September 14: "I overcome obstacles with determination and a positive attitude."
   - Note: Tackle obstacles with unwavering determination and maintain a positive outlook.

Theme: Personal Growth
   - September 15: "I continuously seek to understand myself and the world around me."
   - Note: Embrace a journey of self-discovery and understanding of the world, acknowledging it as a key aspect of personal growth.

Theme: Success
   - September 16: "I define and achieve success on my own terms."
   - Note: Define success in your own terms and strive to achieve it based on your standards and values.

Theme: Mindfulness
   - September 17: "I am present in all my interactions, fostering genuine connections."
   - Note: Focus on being present in your interactions to foster deeper and more genuine connections.

Theme: Motivation
   - September 18: "Every setback is a setup for a comeback. I am ready to rise."
   - Note: View setbacks as setups for stronger comebacks, and

prepare yourself to rise with renewed vigor.

Theme: Personal Growth
   - September 19: "I embrace change as it brings growth and new opportunities."
   - Note: Welcome change as a harbinger of growth and new opportunities in your life.

Theme: Success
   - September 20: "I am confident in my abilities and trust in my journey to success."
   - Note: Have confidence in your abilities and trust in your journey towards achieving success.

Theme: Mindfulness
   - September 21: "I find serenity in the rhythm of my daily routines."
   - Note: Look for serenity and peace in the rhythm and routine of your daily life.

Theme: Motivation
   - September 22: "I am inspired by my visions of the future and motivated to make them a reality."
   - Note: Let your vision of the future inspire and motivate you to turn it into reality.

Theme: Personal Growth
   - September 23: "I am a blend of creativity and logic, constantly growing in harmony."
   - Note: Recognize and nurture the blend of creativity and logic within you, allowing them to grow in harmony.

Theme: Success

- September 24: "My actions today are planting the seeds for tomorrow's success."
- Note: Understand that your actions today are crucial in laying the groundwork for future success.

Theme: Mindfulness

- September 25: "I approach life with a calm mind and a compassionate heart."
- Note: Strive to approach life with calmness and compassion, enriching your experiences and relationships.

Theme: Motivation

-September 26: "I am driven by my inner strength and unwavering commitment."
- Note: Tap into your inner strength and commitment to drive your actions and decisions.

Theme: Personal Growth

- September 27: "I am open to new ideas and experiences that challenge my boundaries."
- Note: Embrace openness to new ideas and experiences that challenge and expand your boundaries.

Theme: Success

- September 28: "I achieve success by aligning my goals with my actions."
- Note: Focus on aligning your goals with your daily actions to create a clear path to success.

Theme: Mindfulness

- September 29: "I cultivate inner peace by connecting with my true self."
- Note: Find inner peace by connecting deeply with your true self and understanding your core values.

Theme: Motivation
- September 30: "My determination is unwavering, even in the face of adversity."
- Note: Maintain a strong sense of determination, especially when facing challenging situations.

This concludes the affirmations for September, each crafted to inspire mindfulness, motivation, personal growth, and a successful mindset. These daily affirmations are intended to guide and support you through various aspects of life, helping to maintain a positive and proactive approach towards personal development and achievements.

October - Balance and Harmony: Encouraging a balanced life, seeking harmony in relationships and personal endeavors

Theme: Personal Growth

- October 1: "Each day brings new opportunities for growth and self-improvement."
- Note: Embrace each day as a new opportunity to grow and improve yourself in different aspects.

Theme: Success

- October 2: "I embrace challenges as they are stepping stones to my success."
- Note: View challenges as opportunities that lead you closer to your success.

Theme: Mindfulness

- October 3: "I am mindful of my mental and physical health, nurturing both with care."
- Note: Pay attention to both your mental and physical health, nurturing each with the care they deserve.

Theme: Motivation

- October 4: "I am motivated by my past victories and future aspirations."
- Note: Draw motivation from your past achievements and future goals.

Theme: Personal Growth

- October 5: "I am adaptable and resilient in the face of

change."
- Note: Cultivate adaptability and resilience, key traits for thriving amidst change.

Theme: Success
- October 6: "I create my own path to success, guided by my values and dreams."
- Note: Be the creator of your own success path, guided by your personal values and aspirations.

Theme: Mindfulness
- October 7: "Today, I choose to live with intention and purpose."
- Note: Make a conscious choice to live each day with clear intention and purpose.

Theme: Motivation
- October 8: "My passion is the key that unlocks my highest potential."
- Note: Recognize your passion as the key to unlocking and realizing your full potential.

Theme: Personal Growth
- October 9: "I am a compilation of my experiences, constantly learning and evolving."
- Note: Understand that you are an ever-evolving being, shaped and enriched by your experiences.

Theme: Success
- October 10: "I attract success by being authentic and true to my principles."

- Note: Believe in the power of authenticity and staying true to your principles to attract success.

Theme: Mindfulness
- October 11: "I find beauty and gratitude in everyday moments."
- Note: Cultivate an attitude of gratitude by finding beauty in the simplicity of everyday life.

Theme: Motivation
- October 12: "I am committed to pursuing my goals with vigor and determination."
- Note: Strengthen your commitment to your goals, approaching them with energy and unwavering determination.

Theme: Personal Growth
- October 13: "I embrace my unique qualities and use them as strengths."
- Note: Recognize and embrace your unique traits, using them as strengths in your journey of personal growth.

Theme: Success
- October 14: "My actions are intentional and steer me towards success."
- Note: Make sure your actions are intentional and aligned with your path to success.

Theme: Mindfulness
- October 15: "I am in harmony with my surroundings, finding peace in the balance of life."
- Note: Strive to be in harmony with your surroundings,

finding peace and balance in life's rhythm.

Theme: Motivation
  - October 16: "I overcome procrastination by focusing on the value and purpose of my tasks."
  - Note: Tackle procrastination by focusing on the importance and purpose behind your tasks.

Theme: Personal Growth
  - October 17: "I continuously push my boundaries to explore new horizons."
  - Note: Challenge yourself to push beyond your comfort zone and explore new possibilities.

Theme: Success
  - October 18: "I am a beacon of creativity and innovation, leading the way to success."
  - Note: Affirm your role as a leader in creativity and innovation, paving the way to success.

Theme: Mindfulness
  - October 19: "I practice kindness and empathy towards myself and others."
  - Note: Emphasize practicing kindness and empathy, both towards yourself and others.

Theme: Motivation
  - October 20: "Every challenge is a new opportunity to showcase my strengths."
  - Note: View challenges as opportunities to demonstrate and strengthen your abilities.

Theme: Personal Growth

- October 21: "I am open to constructive criticism, seeing it as a pathway to growth."
- Note: Embrace constructive feedback as an opportunity for personal development and growth.

Theme: Success

- October 22: "I am confident in my journey, knowing each step brings me closer to success."
- Note: Maintain confidence in your journey, understanding that each step is a progression towards success.

Theme: Mindfulness

- October 23: "I find clarity and focus in moments of quiet reflection."
- Note: Use quiet reflection as a tool to gain clarity and focus in your thoughts and actions.

Theme: Motivation

- October 24: "My dreams are within reach, motivating me to strive for excellence."
- Note: Keep your dreams within sight, letting them motivate you to strive for excellence.

Theme: Personal Growth

- October 25: "I am a masterpiece in progress, embracing both my successes and flaws."
- Note: View yourself as a work in progress, embracing all aspects of your being, including successes and flaws.

Theme: Success

- October 26: "I manifest success by aligning my thoughts and actions with my goals."
- Note: Focus on aligning your thoughts and actions with your goals to manifest success in your life.

Theme: Mindfulness
- October 27: "I approach my day with a calm and centered mind."
- Note: Start your day with a mindset of calmness and centeredness, setting a peaceful tone for what lies ahead.

Theme: Motivation
- October 28: "I am inspired by my visions of the future and act daily to make them a reality."
- Note: Let your vision for the future inspire you to take daily actions towards making it a reality.

Theme: Personal Growth
- October 29: "I value and learn from every experience, growing wiser each day."
- Note: Treat every experience as a learning opportunity, allowing yourself to grow wiser with each new lesson.

Theme: Success
- October 30: "My dedication and hard work lay the ground-work for my success."
- Note: Acknowledge that your dedication and hard work are fundamental to laying the groundwork for your success.

Theme: Mindfulness
- October 31: "I embrace the present, finding magic in the

here and now."

- Note: Especially relevant on Halloween, embrace the present moment and find the magic in the 'here and now'.

These affirmations for October are intended to provide daily guidance and inspiration, focusing on mindfulness, motivation, personal growth, and success. Each affirmation is crafted to encourage a positive mindset and proactive approach to life's challenges and opportunities.

November - Kindness and Compassion: Highlighting the importance of empathy, acts of kindness, and compassion towards others and oneself.

Theme: Motivation
- November 1: "I start this month with renewed energy and a clear vision for my goals."
- Note: Use the start of the month as a time to re-energize and refocus on your vision and goals.

Theme: Personal Growth
- November 2: "I embrace the lessons this time of year brings, growing in wisdom and strength."
- Note: As the year progresses, welcome the unique lessons and growth opportunities it brings.

Theme: Success
- November 3: "I am creating a legacy of success and positivity through my actions."

- Note: Focus on building a legacy of success and positivity with your daily actions and choices.

Theme: Mindfulness

- November 4: "I find stillness and reflection in the quiet moments of autumn."
- Note: Utilize the serene and reflective nature of the autumn season to find stillness and deeper insight.

Theme: Motivation

- November 5: "I am motivated by gratitude for what I have and excitement for what is to come."
- Note: Let gratitude for your current blessings and excitement for the future fuel your motivation.

Theme: Personal Growth

- November 6: "I am a work in progress, constantly evolving and improving."
- Note: Embrace your status as a work in progress, focusing on continuous evolution and self-improvement.

Theme: Success

- November 7: "Success to me means achieving balance and fulfillment in all areas of my life."
- Note: Redefine success as achieving a balance and sense of fulfillment across all aspects of your life.

Theme: Mindfulness

- November 8: "I approach my day with mindfulness, fully engaging in each task and moment."
- Note: Commit to a mindful approach to your day, fully

engaging and being present in every task and moment.

Theme: Motivation
- November 9: "I am driven by my potential to positively impact the world."
- Note: Let the potential for making a positive impact in the world be a key driver of your motivation.

Theme: Personal Growth
- November 10: "I am open to exploring new paths and perspectives, enriching my journey of self-discovery."
- Note: Embrace openness to new paths and perspectives, seeing them as enriching elements of your self-discovery journey.

Theme: Success
- November 11: "I am determined and persistent in the pursuit of my goals, leading to success."
- Note: Affirm your determination and persistence as key factors leading to the successful achievement of your goals.

Theme: Mindfulness
- November 12: "I find contentment and joy in the simplicity of everyday life."
- Note: Seek contentment and joy in the simple aspects of daily life, appreciating the small moments.

Theme: Motivation
- November 13: "I rise above challenges with strength and courage, continually pushing forward."
- Note: Embrace challenges with strength and courage, using them as motivation to keep moving forward.

Theme: Personal Growth

- November 14: "I am committed to personal excellence, striving to be my best self."

- Note: Commit to the pursuit of personal excellence, always striving to be the best version of yourself.

Theme: Success

- November 15: "I celebrate my achievements and use them as stepping stones for future success."

- Note: Take the time to celebrate your achievements, using them as foundations for future successes.

Theme: Mindfulness

- November 16: "I practice patience and understanding, knowing they lead to wiser decisions."

- Note: Cultivate patience and understanding, recognizing their importance in leading to wiser, more informed decisions.

Theme: Motivation

- November 17: "My journey is fueled by a strong sense of purpose and direction."

- Note: Let a clear sense of purpose and direction fuel your journey and daily actions.

Theme: Personal Growth

- November 18: "I embrace both my strengths and weaknesses, knowing they shape my unique character."

- Note: Acknowledge and embrace both your strengths and weaknesses, understanding they collectively shape your unique character.

Theme: Success
   - November 19: "I attract success by staying true to my values and beliefs."
   - Note: Believe in attracting success by remaining true to your core values and beliefs.

Theme: Mindfulness
   - November 20: "I am grateful for the present moment and all it offers."
   - Note: Cultivate gratitude for the present moment and the opportunities it presents.

Theme: Motivation
   - November 21: "I am determined to overcome any obstacle with perseverance and a positive mindset."
   - Note: Affirm your determination to overcome obstacles with perseverance and positivity.

Theme: Personal Growth
   - November 22: "I continuously seek new experiences that broaden my horizons and deepen my understanding."
   - Note: Actively seek out new experiences that expand your horizons and deepen your understanding of the world.

Theme: Success
   - November 23: "My path to success is paved with hard work, dedication, and a clear vision."
   - Note: Recognize that hard work, dedication, and a clear vision are essential in paving your path to success.

Theme: Mindfulness

- November 24: "I am centered and calm, finding peace amidst the day's challenges."
- Note: Strive to remain centered and calm, finding peace even amidst daily challenges.

Theme: Motivation
- November 25: "I am inspired by my progress and motivated to continue my journey with enthusiasm."
- Note: Let the progress you have made be a source of inspiration, motivating you to continue your journey with enthusiasm.

Theme: Personal Growth
- November 26: "I value and respect my journey, embracing each step with courage and optimism."
- Note: Honor and respect your personal journey, embracing each step with courage and a positive outlook.

Theme: Success
- November 27: "I am confident in my abilities and make decisions that lead me to success."
- Note: Have confidence in your abilities and make decisions that steer you towards success.

Theme: Mindfulness
- November 28: "I am mindful of my impact on others, striving to be a positive influence."
- Note: Be aware of your impact on those around you, aiming to be a positive influence in their lives.

Theme: Motivation

- November 29: "My ambitions are the driving force behind my relentless pursuit of excellence."
- Note: Let your ambitions drive your relentless pursuit of excellence in all aspects of
your life.

Theme: Personal Growth
- November 30: "I embrace change as an essential part of my personal evolution and growth."
- Note: View change as an integral and necessary part of your journey towards personal evolution and growth.

These affirmations for November are crafted to provide daily inspiration and guidance, focusing on themes of mindfulness, motivation, personal growth, and success. Each affirmation encourages a positive mindset and proactive approach to life's challenges and opportunities, helping you to maintain focus on your goals and personal well-being.

December - Celebration and Closure: Focusing on celebrating achievements of the year, reflecting on lessons learned, and preparing for the journey ahead.

Theme: Success
- December 1: "I end the year with gratitude for the successes and lessons learned."
- Note: Reflect on the past year with gratitude, appreciating both the successes and the lessons learned.

Theme: Mindfulness
- December 2: "I embrace the winter season with a calm and peaceful heart."
- Note: Welcome the winter season and its unique beauty with a sense of calm and peace.

Theme: Motivation
- December 3: "My aspirations for the new year ignite my motivation and drive."
- Note: Let your aspirations for the upcoming year fuel your motivation and drive.

Theme: Personal Growth
- December 4: "I reflect on my personal growth this year and set intentions for continued development."
- Note: Take time to reflect on your personal growth over the year and set intentions for continued development.

Theme: Success
- December 5: "I celebrate my achievements and set my sights

on even greater successes."

- Note: Celebrate your achievements and look forward to achieving even more in the future.

Theme: Mindfulness

- December 6: "I find joy and serenity in the holiday season, embracing its spirit of giving and love."

- Note: Embrace the holiday season's spirit of joy, giving, and love, finding serenity in these moments.

Theme: Motivation

- December 7: "I am motivated to finish the year strong, laying a foundation for the future."

- Note: Stay motivated to end the year on a strong note, creating a solid foundation for the future.

Theme: Personal Growth

- December 8: "I am open to the lessons this month brings, growing in wisdom and strength."

- Note: Be open to the lessons of December, allowing them to contribute to your wisdom and strength.

Theme: Success

- December 9: "My efforts throughout the year accumulate into significant achievements."

- Note: Recognize that your year-long efforts have culminated in significant achievements.

Theme: Mindfulness

- December 10: "I am present in the festive moments, cherishing time with loved ones."

- Note: Be fully present during the festive season, cherishing the time spent with loved ones.

Theme: Mindfulness
- December 11: "I savor the quiet moments of winter, finding peace in the stillness."
- Note: Embrace the quiet and still moments of winter as opportunities for peace and reflection.

Theme: Motivation
- December 12: "I am driven by the joy and hope this season brings."
- Note: Let the joy and hope characteristic of the season fuel your drive and motivation.

Theme: Personal Growth
- December 13: "I reflect on my year's journey, acknowledging my growth and resilience."
- Note: Take time to reflect on your journey over the year, recognizing your growth and resilience.

Theme: Success
- December 14: "I am grateful for my successes and ready to build on them in the new year."
- Note: Express gratitude for your successes and prepare to build upon them in the coming year.

Theme: Mindfulness
- December 15: "I embrace the festive spirit, finding joy in giving and sharing."
- Note: Embrace the festive spirit of the season, finding joy

in the acts of giving and sharing.

Theme: Motivation
- December 16: "I am inspired to end the year on a positive note, making the most of each day."
- Note: Find inspiration to end the year positively, making the most of each remaining day.

Theme: Personal Growth
- December 17: "I am open to new beginnings and the opportunities they bring."
- Note: Welcome new beginnings and the fresh opportunities they present for growth and discovery.

Theme: Success
- December 18: "I acknowledge my accomplishments and set new goals for the future."
- Note: Acknowledge your accomplishments and set new, challenging goals for the future.

Theme: Mindfulness
- December 19: "I am present in the joy and warmth of the holiday season."
- Note: Stay present and immerse yourself in the joy and warmth that the holiday season brings.

Theme: Motivation
- December 20: "My determination strengthens as the year concludes, looking forward to new challenges."
- Note: Let your determination grow as the year ends, preparing yourself to face new challenges in the coming year with

enthusiasm.

Theme: Personal Growth
  - December 21: "I welcome the winter solstice as a time of reflection and renewal."
  - Note: Use the winter solstice as a time to reflect on the past and renew yourself for future endeavors.

Theme: Success
  - December 22: "I celebrate the year's end as a culmination of my efforts and a bridge to future achievements."
  - Note: View the end of the year as a celebration of your efforts and a stepping stone to future successes.

Theme: Mindfulness
  - December 23: "I find comfort and joy in the simple pleasures of life."
  - Note: Take time to appreciate and find joy in life's simple pleasures during this festive season.

Theme: Motivation
  - December 24: "I am filled with gratitude and inspiration, motivating me to give my best."
  - Note: Let the feelings of gratitude and inspiration during this time motivate you to give your best in all you do.

Theme: Personal Growth
  - December 25: "I cherish the love and connections with family and friends, growing through our shared experiences."
  - Note: Value the time spent with family and friends, recognizing the growth that comes from these connections and

shared experiences.

Theme: Success

- December 26: "I am ready to take on new challenges, paving my path to success in the new year."
- Note: Gear up to face new challenges, paving your way to success in the upcoming year.

Theme: Mindfulness

- December 27: "I reflect on my thoughts and experiences, cultivating mindfulness and understanding."
- Note: Spend time reflecting on your thoughts and experiences to cultivate a deeper sense of mindfulness and understanding.

Theme: Motivation

- December 28: "I am energized by the prospects of a new year and new beginnings."
- Note: Let the prospect of a new year fill you with energy and enthusiasm for new beginnings.

Theme: Personal Growth

- December 29: "I acknowledge my progress and look forward to continuing my journey of self-improvement."
- Note: Acknowledge the progress you've made and look forward to continuing your journey of self-improvement.

Theme: Success

- December 30: "I am proud of what I've achieved this year and excited for what's to come."
- Note: Take pride in your achievements this year and feel

excited for what the future holds.

Theme: Mindfulness
    - December 31: "I bid farewell to this year with gratitude and welcome the new year with hope and enthusiasm."
    - Note: End the year with a sense of gratitude for all that has passed and embrace the new year with hope and enthusiasm.

This concludes the affirmations for December and the year. May these daily affirmations have guided and inspired you throughout the year, providing a source of strength, inspiration, and reflection. As you move forward, remember the power of starting your day with intention and positivity, and may these practices continue to be a valuable part of your journey.

The Power of Daily Affirmations

As we conclude this year-long journey of daily affirmations, it's important to reflect on the transformative power these simple yet profound statements can have on our lives. Starting each day with a specific affirmation sets the tone for our thoughts, actions, and interactions. It's a practice that fosters a positive mindset, strengthens motivation, encourages personal growth, and guides us towards success.

- Mindfulness: Daily affirmations help center our thoughts, bringing our focus back to the present and allowing us to approach the day with calmness and clarity.
    - Motivation: They act as catalysts for motivation, reminding

us of our goals, aspirations, and the drive needed to achieve them.

- Personal Growth: Affirmations encourage continual self-reflection and growth, making us more aware of our progress and areas for improvement.

- Success: By regularly visualizing and affirming our success, we align our mindset and actions with our definitions of

success, thereby attracting and achieving it more readily.

The daily practice of affirmations is more than just repeating positive statements; it's about instilling these affirmations into our subconscious. Over time, this practice helps in shaping our beliefs, attitudes, and behaviors, leading to tangible changes in our lives. It's a tool for self-empowerment and transformation, enabling us to face each day with renewed strength, optimism, and purpose.

As you move forward, remember the power of starting your day with intention and positivity. Whether you continue with these affirmations or create your own, this practice is a valuable part of a mindful, motivated, and growth-oriented lifestyle. Let these affirmations be your daily companions, guiding you towards a fulfilling and successful life.

5

Beyond Affirmations: Sustaining Change

Embracing the Journey of Transformation

In the pursuit of personal growth and change, affirmations are merely the first step, the initial spark that ignites the possibility of transformation. To truly embrace this journey, it's essential to understand the process and commit to sustained actions and shifts in mindset.

- Understanding the Process: Transformation is more than just uttering positive statements; it's about deeply ingraining these affirmations into your daily life. Recognize that true change requires more than words—it demands action, perseverance, and a shift in how you perceive yourself and the world around you. It's a continuous process that involves the evolution of your thoughts, emotions, and behaviors.

- Integrating Lessons: Reflecting on the affirmations used throughout the year is a vital part of this journey. Consider which affirmations resonated with you the most and why. How have these affirmations shifted your perspective, attitudes, or behaviors? Did they help you overcome specific challenges or achieve certain goals? This reflection helps in understanding the impact of affirmations and in identifying the areas where they have catalyzed change.

- The Role of Mindset: Embracing transformation also involves nurturing a growth mindset—a belief that your abilities and intelligence can be developed over time. With this mindset, affirmations become more than just words; they become a belief system that encourages resilience, learning from failures, and viewing challenges as opportunities for growth.

- Commitment to the Journey: Recognize that transformation is a journey, not a destination. It requires an ongoing commitment to self-exploration and self-improvement. This journey might not always be easy; it will have its highs and lows. However, the commitment to persevere, even when faced with obstacles, is what fosters true and lasting change.

In summary, embracing the journey of transformation is about understanding and committing to the process. It's about integrating the lessons learned from affirmations, adopting a growth mindset, and remaining committed to continual self-improvement. This journey, though challenging, is incredibly rewarding, leading to profound personal growth and fulfillment.

Building Sustainable Habits

The journey of transformation is greatly enhanced by the development of sustainable habits. These habits act as the practical embodiment of the affirmations and mindset shifts we strive to achieve. Here's how you can build sustainable habits:

- Consistency is Key: The cornerstone of building sustainable habits is consistency. It's not about making massive changes overnight but about incorporating small, manageable habits into your daily routine. Whether it's dedicating time each morning for meditation, setting aside moments for journaling, or practicing mindfulness exercises, the regularity of these actions is what embeds them into your life.

- Embedding Affirmations into Daily Life: Make your affirmations a living part of your day. This could be through repeating them during a morning routine, using them as mantras during exercise, or reflecting on them during quiet moments. The goal is to move affirmations from a scheduled activity to an integrated part of your daily thought process.

- Setting Achievable Goals: Use the positivity and motivation gained from affirmations to set realistic and achievable goals. Break down these goals into small, actionable steps. Celebrate small victories along the way, as they build momentum and reinforce your commitment.

- Habit Stacking: Incorporate new habits by stacking them onto existing ones. For example, if you already have a morning coffee routine, use that time for reflection or reciting affirmations. By linking new habits to established ones, you're more likely to stick to them.

- Mindful Reminders: Set up reminders that prompt you to practice your new habits. These can be alarms, notes, or visual cues strategically placed in your environment. They serve as gentle nudges to keep you aligned with your new habits.

- Tracking Progress: Keep a habit tracker or journal to monitor your progress. This can be as simple as marking a calendar for each day you successfully practice your new habit or keeping a detailed journal about your experiences and feelings.

Building sustainable habits is a gradual process that requires patience and persistence. By consistently practicing these habits, you reinforce the principles of your affirmations and take concrete steps towards lasting transformation and growth.

Cultivating Mindfulness and Self-Awareness

To truly embody the essence of affirmations and foster sustained change, cultivating mindfulness and self-awareness is essential. This practice involves a deeper understanding of your inner self, your thoughts, and your reactions to the world around you.

- Mindful Practices: Incorporating mindfulness practices into your daily routine is a powerful way to enhance self-awareness. Activities like meditation, yoga, or even mindful walking can help you cultivate a state of presence and awareness. These practices encourage you to experience the present moment fully, without judgment or distraction. They allow you to observe your thoughts and emotions as they are, fostering a deeper understanding of your inner self.

- Self-Reflection: Regular self-reflection is key to cultivating self-awareness. Take time each day to reflect on your thoughts, feelings, and behaviors. Ask yourself questions like, "How did I react to a particular situation?" "What emotions did I feel, and why?" and "Do my actions align with my affirmations and values?" This practice can be enhanced through journaling, providing a space for you to record and process your thoughts and experiences.

- Active Listening to Inner Voice: Develop the habit of listening to your inner voice. This means paying attention to your intuition and the subtle cues your body and mind give you. It's about trusting your instincts and understanding your gut reactions.

- Emotional Intelligence: Work on improving your emotional intelligence. This involves recognizing and understanding your emotions and those of others. It helps in managing emotions effectively, enabling you to respond rather than react to situations.

- Mindful Consumption: Be mindful of the information, media, and conversations you consume. Surround yourself with positivity and resources that align with your values and goals. This helps in maintaining a mindset that supports your affirmations and personal growth.

Cultivating mindfulness and self-awareness is a transformative process. It enhances your understanding of yourself, improves your relationships with others, and aligns your daily life with your true values and intentions. This deepened awareness becomes the foundation upon which sustained change and personal growth are built.

Leveraging Support Systems

An integral part of sustaining change and embedding affirmations into your life involves leveraging support systems. Having a network of support can significantly enhance your journey of transformation by providing encouragement, accountability, and different perspectives.

- Community and Relationships: Build and nurture a supportive community around you. This community can consist of friends, family members, or peers who understand and support your goals. Sharing your journey with them can provide a sense of belonging and encouragement. Engage in meaningful conversations about your aspirations and challenges, and be open to receiving support and offering it in return.

- Professional Guidance: Sometimes, guidance from a professional such as a life coach, therapist, or mentor can be invaluable.

These individuals can offer expert advice, objective insights, and strategies to overcome specific challenges. They can also hold you accountable to your goals and help you navigate through complex emotions or situations.

- Support Groups and Networking: Join support groups or networks that align with your interests or goals. These groups provide a platform to connect with like-minded individuals who can offer motivation, inspiration, and wisdom from their experiences. Participating in workshops, seminars, or online forums can also expand your support network.

- Family and Friends as Pillars of Strength: Don't underestimate the power of support from family and friends. They can provide emotional support, motivation, and a sense of security. Share your goals and progress with them and involve them in your journey where possible.

- Collaboration and Sharing: Collaboration with others can lead to new ideas, shared experiences, and mutual growth. Engage in activities that allow for collaboration, whether it's a joint project, a study group, or a community service activity.

- Utilizing Digital Tools and Online Communities: In today's digital age, online communities and tools can also act as powerful support systems. Participate in online forums, follow motivational social media accounts, or use apps designed for goal setting and habit tracking.

Remember, leveraging support systems isn't a sign of weakness; it's a strategic approach to enriching your journey. These systems provide different perspectives, emotional support, and a sense of community, all of which are crucial for long-term change and personal growth.

Expanding Knowledge and Skills

A critical aspect of sustaining the change initiated by daily affirmations is the continuous expansion of knowledge and skills. This process not only reinforces the affirmations but also equips you with the tools needed for personal and professional growth.

- Continuous Learning: Commit to lifelong learning as a way to continually expand your horizons. This could involve reading books, attending workshops, seminars, or online courses. Choose learning resources that align with your goals and interests. This continuous acquisition of knowledge keeps you informed, inspired, and prepared for new challenges.

- Skill Development: Identify specific skills that will aid in your transformation and seek ways to develop them. For instance, if your affirmations focus on leadership, consider taking courses in communication, team management, or conflict resolution. Skill development can be formal, through courses and certifications, or informal, through self-study and practice.

- Application of Knowledge: Actively apply the knowledge you gain to real-life situations. This practical application helps solidify your learning and gives you a clearer understanding of how theoretical concepts work in practice. It also helps in identifying areas where further learning might be required.

- Learning from Experiences: Recognize that experiences, both good and bad, are valuable learning opportunities. Reflect on your experiences, extract lessons from them, and use these insights to guide your future actions.

- Mentorship and Coaching: Seek mentorship or coaching in areas you wish to excel in. Mentors and coaches can provide invaluable insights, advice, and guidance based on their expertise and experiences.

- Networking for Learning: Engage in networking with professionals and peers in your field of interest. Networking can provide learning opportunities through the exchange of ideas, experiences, and knowledge.

- Keeping Up with Industry Trends: Stay updated with the latest trends and developments in your field. This can be achieved through industry journals, newsletters, conferences, and professional associations. Staying informed helps you remain relevant and adaptive to change.

By continuously expanding your knowledge and skills, you empower yourself to not only achieve but also to exceed your goals. This pursuit of learning and skill development is a lifelong journey that complements and enhances the transformative power of affirmations.

Balancing Self-Compassion with Self-Discipline

Achieving lasting change through affirmations and personal growth requires a delicate balance between self-compassion and self-discipline. This balance is essential for maintaining a healthy and productive journey towards your goals.

- Understanding Self-Compassion: Self-compassion involves treating yourself with the same kindness and understanding that you would offer a good friend. It's about recognizing that setbacks and failures are part of the human experience. When you encounter obstacles or fall short of your expectations, respond with kindness and understanding rather than harsh self-criticism. This approach fosters a supportive internal environment for growth and learning.

- Practicing Self-Compassion: Incorporate practices such as mindfulness, which helps you recognize and accept your current feelings without judgment. When faced with personal challenges, remind yourself that no one is perfect and that you are doing your best. Engage in positive self-talk and affirmations that reinforce self-compassion.

- The Role of Self-Discipline: While self-compassion is nurturing, self-discipline is about setting standards for yourself and striving to meet them. It involves creating routines, setting goals, and sticking to them even when it's challenging. Self-discipline is not about being overly rigid or harsh; it's about creating structure and accountability in your life.

- Cultivating Self-Discipline: Develop a clear plan or routine for your goals, including daily, weekly, or monthly tasks. Use tools like planners, journals, or apps to track your progress and stay organized. Set realistic expectations and deadlines for yourself, and hold yourself accountable for meeting them.

- Balancing the Two: To achieve a balance between self-compassion and self-discipline, recognize when you need to be kind to yourself and when you need to push yourself a little harder. If you find you're being too hard on yourself, ease up and practice self-care. Conversely, if you're being too lenient, refocus on your discipline strategies.

- Growth Mindset: Cultivate a growth mindset, which embraces challenges, perseveres through setbacks, and views effort as a path to mastery. This mindset allows you to be disciplined in your pursuits while being compassionate towards yourself in moments of difficulty.

Balancing self-compassion with self-discipline creates a sustainable approach to personal development. It allows you to grow and progress towards your goals without sacrificing your well-being and mental health. This balance is crucial for long-term success and fulfillment.

Maintaining Long-term Vision

Sustaining change and making the most of daily affirmations require a clear and consistent long-term vision. This vision serves as a guiding light, keeping you aligned with your goals and aspirations, even amidst challenges and distractions.

- Visualize Success: Regular visualization of your goals and what success looks like to you is a powerful tool for maintaining focus. Spend time imagining achieving your goals, the feelings associated with success, and the impact it will have on your life. Visualization not only motivates but also helps in solidifying your long-term vision in your subconscious.

- Goal Setting and Review: Set long-term goals that align with your vision and break them down into smaller, manageable objectives. Regularly review and update your goals to reflect your growth, new insights, and changing circumstances. This continuous process ensures that your goals remain relevant and aligned with your overarching vision.

- Reflecting on Progress: Regular reflection on your progress is crucial. Acknowledge the steps you've taken towards your goals, even the small ones. Reflecting on your journey helps you stay connected to your vision and recognize the growth you've achieved.

- Stay Adaptable: While having a long-term vision is essential, it's equally important to remain flexible. Life can be unpre-dictable, and being adaptable allows you to adjust your goals and strategies in response to changing situations while still keeping your ultimate vision in sight.

- Connecting Daily Actions to Vision: Ensure that your daily actions and decisions are steps towards your long-term vision.

This alignment keeps you grounded and focused, making your daily life a direct contributor to your long-term goals.

- Incorporating Feedback and Learning: Be open to feedback and willing to learn from various sources. Integrating new knowledge and insights can refine your vision, making it more attainable and relevant.

- Celebrating Milestones: Acknowledge and celebrate the milestones you achieve along your journey. These celebrations reinforce your commitment to your vision and provide motivation for the path ahead.

By maintaining a clear long-term vision, you create a sense of purpose and direction in your life. This vision helps to guide your decisions, actions, and priorities, ensuring that the path you are on is one that leads to fulfillment and achievement of your deepest aspirations.

Cementing Change Beyond Affirmations

As we conclude Chapter 4, we stand at a crucial juncture in our journey of personal transformation. This chapter has journeyed beyond the foundational practice of affirmations, delving into the essential strategies for embedding these positive changes deeply and permanently into our lives. It's been an exploration of how to transform the seeds of affirmations into flourishing trees of habits, actions, and sustained change.

This chapter underscored the importance of consistency in embedding affirmations into daily life. It's not just about the affirmations themselves, but about building routines and habits that reinforce their messages. We delved into the significance of making these affirmations a part of our everyday existence, infusing them into our actions, decisions, and perspectives. Such consistency ensures that affirmations are not fleeting thoughts but integral components of our thought processes and, ultimately, our life philosophy.

We also explored the balancing act between self-compassion and self-discipline. While it's crucial to push ourselves towards growth and achievement, it's equally important to practice kindness and understanding towards ourselves, especially during times of challenge or setback. This balance is vital in maintaining motivation and resilience on the path to transformation.

Continuous learning and skill development were highlighted as key elements in supporting the changes brought about by affirmations. Expanding our knowledge and skills not only reinforces our affirmations but also empowers us to tackle new challenges and seize opportunities for growth. This ongoing process of learning keeps us dynamic and adaptable, ready to evolve with our changing goals and environments.

Furthermore, we discussed the importance of leveraging support systems. The journey of personal growth is enriched and often accelerated by the encouragement, wisdom, and accountability provided by others, be it friends, family, mentors, or like-minded communities.

In sum, this chapter has laid out a comprehensive framework for sustaining the positive changes initiated by affirmations. It's a reminder that while affirmations are a powerful starting point, the journey of personal growth is continuous and multifaceted. By committing to these principles and integrating them into our lives, we ensure that the transformation sparked by affirmations becomes a lasting evolution, leading us towards a fulfilling and successful life.

As you move forward from this chapter, carry these insights with you, letting them guide and support your journey towards lasting change and personal mastery.

6

Conclusion

Sustaining Change and Thriving

As we draw this journey to a close, let's take a moment to reflect on the path we have traversed. This book has been more than just about understanding and reciting affirmations; it has been a comprehensive exploration into integrating these powerful statements into the very essence of our daily lives. We have embarked on a path of self-discovery, personal development, and meaningful transformation.

The essence of affirmations lies in their integration into our daily routines and thoughts. This journey has taught us that change is not instantaneous but a gradual process that requires dedication, patience, and a commitment to personal evolution.

As you step beyond the pages of this book, I encourage you to continue embracing affirmations in your everyday life. Let them serve as steadfast guides and sources of inspiration in your ongoing journey. Share your experiences with those around you - friends, family, or online communities. Your story can be a beacon of inspiration for others on similar paths.

If this book has been instrumental in your journey, I would be grateful for your review on Amazon. Your insights and experiences are invaluable, offering guidance and encouragement to others seeking similar transformation.

In conclusion, remember that the journey of affirmations is an ongoing process of speaking, believing, and manifesting. Maintain these practices as you move forward, using them to navigate towards your goals and dreams. Your journey is unique and filled with endless potential and opportunities for growth. Embrace it wholeheartedly, with positivity and resilience.

Thank you for letting me be a part of your transformative journey. Continue to use the power of affirmations to shape your reality, believe in your immense potential, and act towards realizing your dreams. Your journey is a powerful testament to the strength of your intentions and beliefs. May you continue to flourish and succeed in all your endeavors!

Epilogue

As the final words of "365 Daily Affirmations: Cultivating Mindfulness, Motivation, and Success" linger in your mind, it's important to reflect on the journey you have embarked upon. This book was more than a collection of affirmations; it was a companion on a year-long journey of self-discovery and personal growth.

Each day, as you engaged with a new affirmation, you were not just reading words on a page; you were planting seeds of change in the fertile soil of your consciousness. These seeds, watered by your consistent attention and nurtured by your willingness to grow, have begun to sprout. You may have noticed subtle shifts in your thoughts, a new perspective on challenges, or a renewed sense of purpose and joy in your daily life.

The journey you have taken is uniquely yours, marked by its highs and lows, successes and learning moments. Remember, personal growth is not a linear process but an evolving one. The affirmations in this book were stepping stones, guiding you towards a deeper understanding of yourself and your potential.

As you step beyond the pages of this book, carry forward the insights and lessons you have gathered. Let the affirmations continue to be a source of strength and guidance. You have the tools to face life's challenges with resilience and to pursue your dreams with unwavering determination.

I encourage you to look back on this year as a milestone in your journey of self-improvement. Celebrate your progress, no matter how big or small. You have invested in yourself, and that in itself is a remarkable achievement.

The end of this book is not the end of your journey. It's an invitation to continue exploring, growing, and becoming the best version of yourself. May the affirmations you've embraced be the light that guides you on the path ahead, filled with endless possibilities and opportunities for growth.

With warmest regards and best wishes for your continued journey,

Glenn

Afterword

As you turn the final page of "365 Daily Affirmations: Cultivating Mindfulness, Motivation, and Success," I hope you feel a profound sense of accomplishment and anticipation. This book was not just a journey through the year, but a journey into the depths of your own potential and aspirations.

Throughout these pages, each affirmation was carefully chosen to challenge, inspire, and nurture your growth. The journey of self-improvement is an ongoing one, marked by small steps of progress and moments of profound realization. It has been my privilege to accompany you on this path, offering words of encouragement and reflection.

Remember, the power of affirmations lies not only in reading them but in embodying their essence in your daily life. I encourage you to revisit these affirmations, perhaps starting the cycle anew, or turning to specific ones that resonated deeply with you in times of need.

As you move forward, carry with you the lessons and insights you've gained. Allow the affirmations to continue guiding your thoughts and actions towards a life of mindfulness, motivation, and success. The transformation you seek is not just a destination but a continuous journey of evolving and becoming.

I would be honored to hear about your experiences and the changes you've observed in your life. Your stories of growth and transformation are what inspire me to continue this work. Feel free to reach out and share your journey.

Thank you for allowing me the opportunity to be a part of your path to self-discovery and empowerment. May you continue to find strength, peace, and joy in every day.

With heartfelt gratitude and best wishes for your continued journey,

Glenn

About the Author

About the Author

Glenn is an esteemed coach and a devoted advocate for personal transformation, with a rich background in psychology and a deep passion for helping others achieve their fullest potential. Their journey in the realm of personal development spans over a decade, marked by a personal quest to overcome life's challenges and a profound discovery of the transformative power of positive thinking and self-affirmation.

The genesis of "365 Daily Affirmations: Cultivating Mindfulness, Motivation, and Success" can be traced back to Glenn's own practices of daily affirmation and introspection. Observing the significant impact these practices had on their life and those they coached, Glenn was inspired to create a resource that could extend this empowerment to a broader audience.

This book represents the essence of Glenn's years of experience and dedication. It's crafted to be an accessible and powerful tool for individuals at any stage of their personal journey. Glenn holds a firm belief in the power of words to shape thoughts and realities. Through this book, they aspire to provide a daily source of inspiration and empowerment, encouraging readers to cultivate mindfulness, motivation, and success in their lives.

Outside of writing, Glenn engages in many creative endeavors, continually pursuing various forms of self-development. They are passionate about sharing their insights and experiences, contributing to workshops, seminars, and online platforms. "365 Daily Affirmations" is more than a book; it is a testament to Glenn's dedication to fostering growth and fulfillment in the lives of others.

www.ingramcontent.com/pod-product-compliance
Lightning Source LLC
Chambersburg PA
CBHW031423120626
46545CB00006B/2251

* 9 7 8 1 9 6 3 7 8 4 0 0 8 *